F. Ellen Netting, PhD
James W. Ellor, PhD
Editors

Faith-Based Initiatives and Aging Services

Faith-Based Initiatives and Aging Services has been co-published simultaneously as *Journal of Religious Gerontology*, Volume 16, Numbers 1/2 2004.

Pre-publication REVIEWS, COMMENTARIES, EVALUATIONS . . .

"**M**UST READING for leaders of faith-related organizations wishing to partner with government in delivering social services to elders. . . . Highlights important theoretical and practical concerns that relate to President Bush's state-church social service delivery experiment."

Ronald Y. Nakasone, PhD
Director of CenterFaith
Graduate Theological Union
Stanford University Center
for Gerontological Education

The Haworth Pastoral Press®
An Imprint of The Haworth Press, Inc.

New York • London • Victoria (AU)
www.HaworthPress.com

Faith-Based Initiatives and Aging Services

Faith-Based Initiatives and Aging Services has been co-published simultaneously as *Journal of Religious Gerontology,* Volume 16, Numbers 1/2 2004.

The *Journal of Religious Gerontology*™ Monographic "Separates" (formerly *Journal of Religion & Aging*)*

Below is a list of "separates," which in serials librarianship means a special issue simultaneously published as a special journal issue or double-issue *and* as a "separate" hardbound monograph. (This is a format which we also call a "DocuSerial.")

"Separates" are published because specialized libraries or professionals may wish to purchase a specific thematic issue by itself in a format which can be separately cataloged and shelved, as opposed to purchasing the journal on an on-going basis. Faculty members may also more easily consider a "separate" for classroom adoption.

"Separates" are carefully classified separately with the major book jobbers so that the journal tie-in can be noted on new book order slips to avoid duplicate purchasing.

You may wish to visit Haworth's website at . . .

http://www.HaworthPress.com

. . . to search our online catalog for complete tables of contents of these separates and related publications.

You may also call 1-800-HAWORTH (outside US/Canada: 607-722-5857), or Fax 1-800-895-0582 (outside US/Canada: 607-771-0012), or e-mail at:

docdelivery@haworthpress.com

Faith-Based Initiatives and Aging Services, edited by F. Ellen Netting, PhD, and James W. Ellor, PhD (Vol. 16, No. 1/2, 2004). *A guide to the key issues in the development and implementation of faith-based programs as defined by both community agencies and the Center for Faith-Based and Community Initiatives.*

Practical Theology for Aging, edited by Rev. Derrel R. Watkins, PhD (Vol. 15, No. 1/2, 2003). *"THOUGHT-PROVOKING, ENLIGHTENING, INSIGHTFUL, AND PRACTICAL. As I read through the book, I repeatedly found myself thinking, 'what AN EXCELLENT SUPPLEMENTAL TEXT for the Introduction to Gerontology course.' AN EXCELLENT TRAINING RESOURCE for health care providers working with older adults, as well as religious leaders of all denominations as they seek to enhance their pastoral care programs with older adults."* (*Patricia Gleason-Wynn, PhD, Lecturer, School of Social Work, Baylor University*)

New Directions in the Study of Late Life Religiousness and Spirituality, edited by Susan H. McFadden, PhD, Mark Brennan, PhD, and Julie Hicks Patrick, PhD (Vol. 14, No. 1, 2/3, 2003). *"Refreshing. . . . encouraging. . . . This book has given us a gift of evolving thoughts and perspectives on religion and spirituality in the later years of life. . . . Of interest not only to university students, researchers, and scholars, but also to those who provide services to the aged." (James Birren, PhD, Associate Director, UCLA Center on Aging)*

Aging Spirituality and Pastoral Care: A Multi-National Perspective, edited by Rev. Elizabeth MacKinlay, RN, PhD, Rev. James W. Ellor, PhD, DMin, DCSW, and Rev. Stephen Pickard, PhD (Vol. 12, No. 3/4, 2001). *"Comprehensive . . . The authors are not just thinkers and scholars. They speak from decades of practical expertise with the aged, demented, and dying." (Bishop Tom Frame, PhD, Lecturer in Public Theology, St. Mark's National Theological Centre, Canberra, Australia)*

Religion and Aging: An Anthology of the Poppele Papers, edited by Derrel R. Watkins, PhD, MSW, MRE (Vol. 12, No. 2, 2001). *"Within these pages, the new ministry leader is supplied with the core prerequisites for effective older adult ministry and the more experienced leader is provided with an opportunity to reconnect with timeless foundational principles. Insights into the interior of the aging experience, field-tested and proven techniques and ministry principles, theological rationale for adult care giving, Biblical perspectives on aging, and philosophic and spiritual insights into the aging process." (Dennis R. Myers, LMSW-ACP, Director, Baccalaureate Studies in Social Work, Baylor University, Waco, Texas)*

Aging in Chinese Society: A Holistic Approach to the Experience of Aging in Taiwan and Singapore, edited by Homer Jernigan and Margaret Jernigan (Vol. 8, No. 3, 1992). *"A vivid introduction to aging in these societies. . . . Case studies illustrate the interaction of religion, personality, immigration, modernization, and aging." (Clinical Gerontologist)*

Spiritual Maturity in the Later Years, edited by James J. Seeber (Vol. 7, No. 1/2, 1991). *"An excellent introduction to the burgeoning field of gerontology and religion."* (*Southwestern Journal of Theology*)

Gerontology in Theological Education: Local Program Development, edited by Barbara Payne and Earl D. C. Brewer* (Vol. 6, No. 3/4, 1989). *"Directly relevant to gerontological education in other contexts and to applications in the educational programs and other work of church congregations and community agencies for the aging."* (*The Newsletter of the Christian Sociological Society*)

Gerontology in Theological Education, edited by Barbara Payne and Earl D. C. Brewer* (Vol. 6, No. 1/2, 1989). *"An excellent resource for seminaries and anyone interested in the role of the church in the lives of older persons . . . must for all libraries."* (*David Maldonado, DSW, Associate Professor of Church & Society, Southern Methodist University, Perkins School of Theology*)

Religion, Aging and Health: A Global Perspective, compiled by the World Health Organization, edited by William M. Clements* (Vol. 4, No. 3/4, 1989). *"Fills a long-standing gap in gerontological literature. This book presents an overview of the interrelationship of religion, aging, and health from the perspective of the world's major faith traditions that is not available elsewhere . . . "* (*Stephen Sapp, PhD, Associate Professor of Religious Studies, University of Miami, Coral Gables, Florida*)

New Directions in Religion and Aging, edited by David B. Oliver* (Vol. 3, No. 1/2, 1987). *"This book is a telescope enabling us to see the future. The data of the present provides a solid foundation for seeing the future."* (*Dr. Nathan Kollar, Professor of Religious Studies and Founding Chair, Department of Gerontology, St. John Fisher College; Adjunct Professor of Ministerial Theology, St. Bernard's Institute*)

The Role of the Church in Aging, Volume 3: Programs and Services for Seniors, edited by Michael C. Hendrickson* (Vol. 2, No. 4, 1987). *Experts explore an array of successful programs for the elderly that have been implemented throughout the United States in order to meet the social, emotional, religious, and health needs of the elderly.*

The Role of the Church in Aging, Volume 2: Implications for Practice and Service, edited by Michael C. Hendrickson* (Vol. 2, No. 3, 1986). *"Filled with important insight and state-of-the-art concepts that reflect the cutting edge of thinking among religion and aging professionals."* (*Rev. James W. Ellor, DMin, AM, CSW, ACSW, Associate Professor, Department Chair, Human Service Department, National College of Education, Lombard, Illinois*)

The Role of the Church in Aging, Volume 1: Implications for Policy and Action, edited by Michael C. Hendrickson* (Vol. 2, No. 1/2, 1986). *Reviews the current status of the religious sector's involvement in the field of aging and identifies a series of strategic responses for future policy and action.*

Published by

The Haworth Pastoral Press, 10 Alice Street, Binghamton, NY 13904-1580 USA

The Haworth Pastoral Press is an imprint of The Haworth Press, Inc., 10 Alice Street, Binghamton, NY 13904-1580 USA.

Faith-Based Initiatives and Aging Services has been co-published simultaneously as *Journal of Religious Gerontology*^{TM}, Volume 16, Numbers 1/2 2004.

The development, preparation, and publication of this work has been undertaken with great care. However, the publisher, employees, editors, and agents of The Haworth Press and all imprints of The Haworth Press, Inc., including The Haworth Medical Press® and Pharmaceutical Products Press®, are not responsible for any errors contained herein or for consequences that may ensue from use of materials or information contained in this work. Opinions expressed by the author(s) are not necessarily those of The Haworth Press, Inc.

Cover design by Kerry E. Mack

Library of Congress Cataloging-in-Publication Data

Faith-based initiatives and aging services / F. Ellen Netting, and James W. Ellor, editors.
     p. cm.
     "Faith-based initiatives and aging services has been co-published simultaneously as Journal of religious gerontology, volume 16, numbers 1/2 2004."
     Includes bibliographical references and index.
     ISBN 0-7890-2733-X (hard cover : alk. paper)–ISBN 0-7890-2734-8 (pbk : alk. paper)
     1. Aging–Religious aspects–Christianity. 2. Older Christians–Religious life. 3. Church work with older people. 4. Church charities–United States. 5. Human services–United States. 6. Church and state–United States. I. Netting, F. Ellen. II. Ellor, James W. III. Journal of religious gerontology.
BV4580.F24 2005
201'.7626'0973–dc22
                                               2004017174

Faith-Based Initiatives and Aging Services

F. Ellen Netting, PhD
James W. Ellor, PhD
Editors

Faith-Based Initiatives and Aging Services has been co-published simultaneously as *Journal of Religious Gerontology*, Volume 16, Numbers 1/2 2004.

The Haworth Pastoral Press®
An Imprint of The Haworth Press, Inc.

New York • London • Victoria (AU)
www.HaworthPress.com

Indexing, Abstracting & Website/Internet Coverage

This section provides you with a list of major indexing & abstracting services and other tools for bibliographic access. That is to say, each service began covering this periodical during the year noted in the right column. Most Websites which are listed below have indicated that they will either post, disseminate, compile, archive, cite or alert their own Website users with research-based content from this work. (This list is as current as the copyright date of this publication.)

Abstracting, Website/Indexing Coverage . . . . Year When Coverage Began

- *Abstracts in Social Gerontology: Current Literature on Aging* **1991**
- *AgeInfo CD-Rom* **1994**
- *AgeLine Database <http://research.aarp.org/ageline>* **1994**
- *Applied Social Sciences Index & Abstracts (ASSIA)*
    (Online: ASSI via Data-Star) (CD-Rom: ASSIA Plus)
    <http://www.csa.com> **1994**
- *ATLA Religion Database with ATLASerials. This periodical is*
    indexed in ATLA Religion Database with ATLASerials,
    published by the American Theological Library
    Association <http://www.atla.com/> **1991**
- *AURSI African Urban & Regional Science Index. A scholarly &*
    research index which synthesizes & compiles all publications
    on urbanization & regional science in Africa within the world.
    Published annually. **2004**
- *Christian Periodical Index <http://www.acl.org/cpl.htm>* **1995**
- *Educational Administration Abstracts (EAA)* **1995**
- *Family & Society Studies Worldwide (online and CD/ROM)*
    <http://www.nisc.com> **1996**
- *Family Index Database <http://www.familyscholar.com>* **1995**
- *Guide to Social Science & Religion in Periodical Literature* **2000**
- *Human Resources Abstracts (HRA)* **1991**
- *IBZ International Bibliography of Periodical Literature*
    <http://www.saur.de> **1996**

(continued)

Special Bibliographic Notes related to special journal issues (separates) and indexing/abstracting:

- indexing/abstracting services in this list will also cover material in any "separate" that is co-published simultaneously with Haworth's special thematic journal issue or DocuSerial. Indexing/abstracting usually covers material at the article/chapter level.
- monographic co-editions are intended for either non-subscribers or libraries which intend to purchase a second copy for their circulating collections.
- monographic co-editions are reported to all jobbers/wholesalers/approval plans. The source journal is listed as the "series" to assist the prevention of duplicate purchasing in the same manner utilized for books-in-series.
- to facilitate user/access services all indexing/abstracting services are encouraged to utilize the co-indexing entry note indicated at the bottom of the first page of each article/chapter/contribution.
- this is intended to assist a library user of any reference tool (whether print, electronic, online, or CD-ROM) to locate the monographic version if the library has purchased this version but not a subscription to the source journal.
- individual articles/chapters in any Haworth publication are also available through the Haworth Document Delivery Service (HDDS).

Dedication

The Reverend Doctor Donald F. Clingan

This volume is dedicated to the late Reverend Dr. Donald F. Clingan. Dr. Clingan was an ordained minister of the Christian Church (Disciples of Christ) who served as the founding president and first executive director of the National Interfaith Coalition on Aging.

While serving as a parish pastor and nursing home chaplain in 1980, I met Dr. Clingan who was then the executive director of the National Center on Ministry with the Aging, sponsored by the National Benevolent Association of the Christian Church (Disciples of Christ), and the Christian Theological Seminary, Indianapolis, Indiana. In this capacity, he was conducting a seminar on ministry with the aging for his denomination in Lemoyne, Pennsylvania. As a student of religion and aging, I attended his seminar and was drawn to and energized by his vision, wisdom, and expertise in older adult ministries. Over time Dr. Clingan became my friend and mentor. He had a wonderful gift of helping church leaders gain insight and understanding into the problems and complexities of our aging society. He was particularly concerned about the "spiritual well-being" of older adults in our religious faith communities.

With the recent death of Dr. Clingan, we have lost an encourager whose words lifted us; a mentor whose wisdom guided us; and a friend whose understanding graced us. May our work and ministry never fail to touch the lives of God's "splendid ones" and to further their "spiritual well-being."

Rev. Dr. Richard H. Gentzler, Jr.
Director, Center on Aging and Older Adult Ministries
General Board of Discipleship of The United Methodist Church
Nashville, TN

Faith-Based Initiatives and Aging Services

CONTENTS

ABOUT THE EDITORS

F. Ellen Netting, PhD, ACSW, is Professor of Social Work at Virginia Commonwealth University (VCU) where she teaches in the BSW, MSW, and PhD programs in the area of macro practice, policy, administration, and planning. She has been at VCU for 12 years, having previously taught 10 years at Arizona State University. She continues to collaborate with Dr. Peter M. Kettner and Dr. Steven L. McMurtry on Social Work Macro Practice now in its third edition (2003) with Allyn & Bacon. In addition, she is the co-author of six additional books and has published over 100 book chapters and refereed journal articles. She received the VCU Distinguished Scholar Award in 1997 and was elected to the National Academy of Social Work Practice as a Distinguished Scholar in 1998. Her scholarship has focused on health and human service delivery issues for frail elders, as well as nonprofit management concerns, primarily in religiously affiliated agencies. Recently she completed a project funded by The John A. Hartford Foundation as part of a national demonstration on primary care physician practice in geriatrics, in conjunction with an interdisciplinary team of researchers. Currently, she is part of a national project funded by The Pew Charitable Trusts and located at Baylor University that is studying faith-based programs. She serves on the editorial boards of *Journal of Religious Gerontology, Nonprofit Management and Leadership, Journal of Community Practice,* and *Journal of Gerontological Social Work* and reviews articles for numerous journals in the areas of social work, nonprofit management, and aging.

James W. Ellor, PhD, DMin, LCSW, ACSW, BCD, DCSW,CGP, is the Director of the Institute for Gerontological Studies at Baylor University School of Social Work. Previously he was Professor of Gerontology and Director of the Center for Positive Aging at National-Louis University for twenty years. He is the Editor of *Journal of Religious Gerontology* and Editor-in-Chief of Pastoral Press at the Haworth Press. His recent books include: McKinlay, Elizabeth, James Ellor, and

Stephen Pickard (2002) *Aging, Spirituality and Pastoral Care in the Twenty-First Century: A Multi-National Perspective* (Binghamton: The Haworth Press). This book is edited with two Australian colleagues and contains authors from England, New Zealand, the United States and Australia. He is editor of Ellor, J., McFadden, S., and Sapp, S. (1999) *Tenth Anniversary Issue: Aging and Spirituality* (San Francisco: American Society on Aging); and has collaborated on Ellor, J., McGilliard, J., and Schroeder, P. (1994) *Leading a Congregation in the Aging: Clergy Training Manual* (Washington DC National Council on the Aging) and on Ellor, J., Netting, E., and Thibault, J. (1999) *Understanding Religious and Spiritual Aspects of Human Service Practice* (Columbia: The University of South Carolina Press). He co-edited Kimble, M., McFadden, S.H., Ellor, J.W., and Seeber, J.S. (1995) *Aging, Religion, and Spirituality: A Handbook* (Minneapolis: Fortress Press).

Preface

James W. Ellor, PhD

Persons who work in the community know that religious congregations and Faith-Based Organizations (FBOs) have been working on behalf of the needs of older adults for hundreds of years. Biblically mandated, these services have often defined the "deserving poor" as widows and orphans, and they have been the motivations for religious congregations from the Jewish, Christian and Islamic traditions to work with seniors. Clearly, this is not the exclusive territory of these faith traditions, but surveys have suggested that most faith traditions are drawn to the support of their older members, as well as other persons in their more immediate communities.

In this volume, the editors have worked to capture this activity as it has more recently evolved. Since the early years of President Reagan's administration in the United States, researchers have studied the role of religious congregations in providing services. This text focuses on the specific applications of these services with older adults. The editors, Drs. Netting and Ellor, initiated this volume, by interviewing Elizabeth Seale-Scott, then Director of the Center for Faith-Based and Community Initiatives in the U. S. Department of Health and Human Services. While older adults have perhaps not been the principle focus of this Department, clearly the work of the Administration on Aging has been carried out under its domain. This interview is contained within this volume.

[Haworth co-indexing entry note]: "Preface." Ellor, James W. Co-published simultaneously in *Journal of Religious Gerontology* (The Haworth Pastoral Press, an imprint of The Haworth Press, Inc.) Vol. 16, No. 1/2, 2004, pp. xxiii-xxiv; and: *Faith-Based Initiatives and Aging Services* (eds: F. Ellen Netting, and James W. Ellor) The Haworth Pastoral Press, an imprint of The Haworth Press, Inc., 2004, pp. xv-xvi. Single or multiple copies of this article are available for a fee from The Haworth Document Delivery Service [1-800-HAWORTH, 9:00 a.m. - 5:00 p.m. (EST). E-mail address: docdelivery@haworthpress.com].

xv

The articles within this volume begin with a focus on the "Separation of Church and State," followed by "Micro Practice and Faith-Based Initiatives" in which the role of religious congregations are explored. A more macro practice perspective by Dr. Netting then focuses on "Faith-Related Agencies and Their Implications for Aging Services." The next article offers an edited transcript of the dialogue with Ms. Seale-Scott, in an effort to help define the efforts of her office to work for older adults. This article is followed by the perspectives of individuals from two faith traditions. A Baptist perspective is provided by Dr. Singletary and a Volunteers of America perspective is offered by Ron Field. Concerns around older volunteers and management of faith-based-organizations is addressed by Nancy Macduff, and is followed by a view of faith organizations and ethnically diverse elders by Drs. Tirrito and Choi. It is hoped that these resources will support the work of readers in the community as well as institutions in their work with older adults.

The final section of this volume offers an historical perspective on the field of religion, spirituality and aging in the article, "The Heritage of Religion and Spirituality in the Field of Gerontology."

It is fitting that this volume that has worked to address both theory and practice should be dedicated to Donald F. Clingan, one of the founders of the National Interfaith Coalition on Aging and a key player in two White House Conferences on Aging. Don dedicated his life to addressing the religious needs of older adults, as a pastor, administrator, and author.

Separation of Church and State: Impact on Faith-Based Services

James W. Ellor, PhD

SUMMARY. Legal advocates, clergy and politicians have all been challenged by the concept of the separation of church and state since the first European set foot on the American continent. Two schools of thought have been developed for this unique problem in the United States. Roger Williams took the position that there needs to be a separation of church and state in order to keep the church pure from the politics and every day work of the state. Thomas Jefferson, who is often attributed with developing this concept, took the position that the need for this separation was to protect the state from the church. Both positions often get articulated as if they are one concept in the United States. However, they are very different. This debate has carried itself in the current millennium into the work of the Office of Faith-Based Initiatives as well as the legislation known as Charitable Choice. *[Article copies available for a fee from The Haworth Document Delivery Service: 1-800-HAWORTH. E-mail address: <docdelivery@haworthpress.com> Website: <http://www.HaworthPress.com> © 2004 by The Haworth Press, Inc. All rights reserved.]*

Rev. James W. Ellor is Director of the Institute of Gerontological Studies, Baylor University School of Social Work, One Bear Place #97320, Waco, TX 76798-7320. He is also an Associate Director of the Center for Aging, Religion and Spirituality, St. Paul, MN (E-mail: James_Ellor@Baylor.Edu).

[Haworth co-indexing entry note]: "Separation of Church and State: Impact on Faith-Based Services." Ellor, James W. Co-published simultaneously in *Journal of Religious Gerontology* (The Haworth Pastoral Press, an imprint of The Haworth Press, Inc.) Vol. 16, No. 1/2, 2004, pp. 1-13; and: *Faith-Based Initiatives and Aging Services* (ed: F. Ellen Netting, and James W. Ellor) The Haworth Pastoral Press, an imprint of The Haworth Press, Inc., 2004, pp. 1-13. Single or multiple copies of this article are available for a fee from The Haworth Document Delivery Service [1-800-HAWORTH, 9:00 a.m. - 5:00 p.m. (EST). E-mail address: docdelivery@haworthpress.com].

http://www.haworthpress.com/web/JRG
© 2004 by The Haworth Press, Inc. All rights reserved.
Digital Object Identifier: 10.1300/J078v16n01_01

KEYWORDS. Jefferson, Williams, separation of church and state, Charitable Choice, Faith-Based Initiatives, religion

"Religious tolerance, that is a big part of the Cause. . . . Every group wants tolerance for themselves, . . . but in practice it would seem that there are so many groups wanting that, that the end result shall have to be universal tolerance" (Nelson, 2000. pp. 242-243). The popular conception of the Revolutionary War in the United States is that one of the freedoms that patriots were fighting for was freedom of religion. This quote from a fictional discussion between two revolutionaries reflects a perception of a twentieth century author on an eighteenth century ideal. Like most cultural myths, the historic record suggests a somewhat more complex picture. Ironically, it can be argued that much of the sentiment at the time was not freedom of religion for everyone, but rather freedom for one's own perspective.

The first amendment freedom of religion has been mythologized to be understood to mean that there is a clear separation of church and state. Freedom of religion and the separation of church and state are somewhat different. Like most other public policies these two concepts find root in law, yet their application to any given context is a matter of judgment and executive policy. This separation has also been constantly interpreted by the judicial system in this country (Lupu & Tuttle, 2002).

The history of the separation of church and state reflects a diversity of different philosophical positions and agendas. Often in this dialogue, two positions are reflected. On the one hand, it refers to the theological need to protect the church from the laws of the state. On the other hand, it reflects the philosophical need to protect the state from the influence of the church. In the current discourse around Faith-Based Initiatives, the decedents of each of these positions have taken aim at both the White House Office for Faith-Based and Community Initiatives as well as the loosely related Charitable Choice legislation. In order to better understand the assumed root of the White House Office for Faith-Based and Community Initiatives as well as the Charitable Choice legislation, this article will reflect on the history of this philosophical concept in the United States.

SEPARATION OF CHURCH AND STATE

The separation of church and state is best understood when examined from three different perspectives. First, this separation is a part of the history of the United States as a function of the theologies of some of the early settlers. Second, it is reflected in the philosophy of the signers of the U. S. Constitution, particularly Thomas Jefferson. Finally, it has taken shape as an historical tool for legislation and public policy. Interpreters of the current political and legislative agendas, whether or not they are conscious of it, stand on these three platforms to carry out both policy analyses and interpretations.

Theological Interpretation

The fundamental question that theologians posit rests on the manner in which believers are to respond to civil and religious authorities. Theologians point out that civil authority is different from that of religion. Civil authority regulates social interactions of this world. It is up to government to be sure that the things of this world, such as roads, communication and even the taxes that are levied to pay for them are in good order. Religions, on the other hand, focus on the nature of, and interaction with, God. This does not suggest that the two are mutually exclusive. In fact, among the world's religious traditions, a larger number would not recognize this split than would see it as relevant. However, when the two are separate, there are numerous potential conflicts. For example, what if civil authority mandates something like service in the army when to the believer this is against his or her religion. Is the individual believer protected from what is otherwise a universal mandate? Conscientious objectors were as visible in the Revolutionary War as they were in the Viet Nam conflict. This becomes more personal when it comes to such issues as abortion or blood transfusions. Throughout the recent centuries of United States history, such issues as land ownership, adultery and rape have also been publically mandated. To one person a legal definition of abortion is an appropriate protection of life. But, to another, it is an infringement on the rights of the mother. The more fundamental question is: does civil law have the authority to make such a decision of conscience? At the heart of the debate as to civil versus religious authority is the passage found in Greek Scripture, Luke 20:25 "Render therefore unto Caesar the things which be Caesar's, and unto God the things which be God's."

One side of the debate is historically supplied by protestant theology and predates the U. S. Constitution by many years. In this concept, the faithful are viewed as a symbol of purity in an unclean world. This metaphor dates back to the protestant reformation of the 15th and 16th centuries. Pivotal to this position is the book of John chapter 18 verse 36, Jesus said, "My kingdom is not of this world." Martin Luther based in part his concept that "differentiated between the 'two kingdoms, one the kingdom of God, the other the kingdom of the world'" (Hamburger, 2002. p. 22) on this passage. John Calvin also felt that these two should always be examined separately (Hamburger, 2002. p. 22). Yet, each of these two protestant reformers meant something slightly different. Luther understood the two to be separate but brought together by the human experience. Calvin felt that scripture offers a clear guideline on this. In his commentary on the Luke passage, he notes that this passage, "lays down a clear distinction between spiritual and civil governments" (Calvin 1993. p. 44). Calvin goes on to say that "Christ reckoned it enough to draw a distinction between the spiritual kingdom of God, on the one hand, and political order and the condition of the present life, on the other" (Calvin, 1993. p. 45). Calvin understood that God alone was the lawgiver for governing souls and the one who sets the rules for worship, but as long as the activities of government do not hinder this worship, they should be administered by the princes or civil authorities. He makes it clear, however, that where the two conflict, God's law is superior and to be enforced.

In the interpretations of Luther or Calvin, the crucial element is found in the purity of church in relationship with God, both as institution and as a reflection of the human heart. Hamburger notes, "during the Reformation Protestants relied upon the contrast between these jurisdictions in their arguments against the Catholic Church, and eventually dissenting Protestants employed this contrast to challenge Protestant establishments" (Calvin, 1993. p. 45). In the sixteenth century, the Anabaptists withdrew from worldly affairs stating that "A separation shall be made from the evil and from the wickedness which the devil planted in the world; in this manner, simply that we shall not have fellowship with them [the wicked] and not run with them in the multitude of their abominations" (Calvin, 1993. p. 45). Invoking the image of the Garden of Eden, this argument suggests that the church be separated from the state in order to maintain the sanctity of the church. Within the Anabaptist tradition, the purpose was to actually separate the individual from all affairs of the state. Thus, Anabaptists separated themselves from all public office and all worldly affairs of the State. This was not true of all

Protestants in this era. Hamburger notes that the overwhelming number of Protestants felt that there should be some connection between church and state in that they prayed for those in government service and taught obedience to the law. The general feeling was simply that the two should be run by different people (Hamburger, 2002. p. 28). It is, however, from this image of the garden separating the Christian from the evils of the world that the concept of a wall, or garden wall, of separation seems to have emanated. Often citing both the Genesis story of the Garden of Eden and the Song of Songs 4:12 account of an enclosed garden, the wall was a defense for the good against the evils of this world.

The image of the wall of separation between church and state is often attributed to Thomas Jefferson. However it is clearly in evidence as a symbol in the work of an earlier writer, Roger Williams, one of the founders of the State of Rhode Island. To Roger Williams, the wall divided the "godly and the profane" (Hamburger, 2002. p. 5). Roger Williams was a Separatist. Separatists feared governments and communities in the new world would include both sinners and those who were repentant of their sins. Unlike Anglicans and congregationalists who saw that the entire nation had a covenant with God, separatists felt that there was a profound need to maintain the purity of the church and thus believers. Williams would seem to have been a separatist from even the puritan separatists. It is understood that he went so far as to preach that "a man should not pray with his wife if she were unregenerate" (Hamburger, 2002. p. 40). The emphasis in the theology of Roger Williams was on maintaining the purity of the church. Williams was also not in favor of a strong clergy. He felt that the purity of the church was best maintained by the counsel of believers. Built on Calvin's concept that while each individual has sinned and thus fallen short of the glory of God, the spirit is able to work within groups of people. In effect, Calvin was saying that what we would today refer to as the group dynamic is less defiled by the sinful nature of the individual, and thus a more pure vehicle for the holy spirit to speak to humanity. Williams was concerned that a strong clergy such as that found in the Massachusetts Colony could be corrupted too easily by the human elements of the individuals involved.

The Christian tradition based on Luke 20:25, "Render therefore unto Caesar the things which be Caesar's, and unto God the things which be God's" creates the potential for a unique separation that is not found as clearly within the other world religions. In the creation of the first amendment to the U.S. Constitution, this concept was used to reject the adoption of a specific religion by any governmental body. During the time of the Revolution the colony of Virginia, for example, had adopted the Anglican religion as the religion of the state. Salaries of Anglican clergy were paid out of state monies, but not those of other religious traditions. Thus, persons from other religious traditions paid the salary of the Anglican pastor through their taxes and then still had to tithe to support their own congregations. These arguments were also used to support the various protestant traditions in their arguments against the governance of the Roman Catholic tradition.

Paradoxically, within this argument, the so-called wall of separation, that was conceived by Williams between church and state, was understood to maintain the purity of the church. To the extent that the rules of the church and state conflicted, this position recognizes that the rules of the church should prevail. Implications for conscientious objection for example, as well as such things as blood transfusions, are clear. Where there is conflict, the rules of the church prevail.

Freedom from Religion

Prior to the Revolution, many of the states had been settled by specific religious groups, many of whom left Europe to be able to practice their specific faith tradition. In this country, as the colonies were developed, they moved from communities of faith to larger municipalities. With the development of local and colonial governments also came the need to protect the original faith tradition. Several states had adopted specific faith traditions as the official religion of that colony. Massachusetts had selected the congregational tradition, Maryland the Roman Catholic tradition and Virginia the Anglican tradition, to name a few. Prior to the revolution, many states not only actively supported one religious tradition, they often had laws against practicing other traditions. One of the specific points of conflict between the various faith traditions came in both the French and Indian and the Revolutionary wars regarding sending men to fight. The Presbyterians in this instance were often frustrated by the Quakers for not sending men to help defend the Pennsylvania Colony from Indian Raids. Some states also went so far as to bar persons from other faith traditions from holding public office. However, by the end of the Revolution, most colonies had dropped these laws. While some privileges remained for persons from the majority religions, the practice of the various religious traditions was more fully tolerated.

As the work of the framers of the Constitution and subsequently what came to be known as the Bill of Rights was progressing, the nature of this relationship continued to be discussed. One position offered by a number of religious traditions, particularly the Presbyterians, suggested that civil government's involvement in religion should be restricted to allowing all religions to worship in accordance with their own tradition. In other words, the role of civil religion is to protect the rights of religious expression by the various churches.

As the author of the first amendment, Thomas Jefferson is generally credited with the development of what would emerge as the language of law on religious freedom. Jefferson's position started on the opposite side of the wall of separation between church and state from that of Roger Williams. His position was that it is the state that must be protected from the church. Jefferson first articulated his position in the only book that he ever wrote, entitled *Notes on the State of Virginia* (Jefferson, 1982. p. 157-161), first published in 1787. Jefferson starts out his discussion by pointing out that "several acts of the Virginia assembly of 1659, 1662 and 1693, had made it penal in parents to refuse to have their children baptized" (Jefferson, 1982. p. 157). In this section of his *Notes to the State of Virginia*, Jefferson makes it clear that he feels that the citizens of the state have been encumbered by the dominant religion. In the case of the State of Virginia, it was the Anglican Tradition.

Jefferson notes that the Virginia State convention of 1776 "repealed all acts of parliament which had rendered criminal the maintaining any opinions in matters of religion" (Jefferson, 1982. p. 158). Only the local ordinances or Virginia Commonwealth laws remained in this area. His argument goes on to note that government does not prescribe what medicines one is to take nor in which diet to engage. He suggests that one's soul should be as free for self-expression as one's body. Jefferson uses the analogy that two people are simply not at all the same size. To try to make them all the same, we would have to cut off parts of some and stretch parts of others. In this same way, people cannot be the same in terms of their religious expression. In fact, "difference of opinion is advantageous in religion" (Jefferson, 1982. p. 160).

Jefferson himself recognized the need to be a free thinker when it came to his own understanding of religion. He defined religion in the preface to the Jefferson Bible as, "our human response to the dual reality of being alive and having to die" (Jefferson, 1989). Jefferson subtitles his Bible with the phrase, "the life and morals of Jesus of Nazareth" (Jefferson, 1989). A brief reading of this text reveals to the reader that he has taken the synoptic gospels (Matthew, Mark and Luke), integrated them together and deleted any reference to the divinity of Jesus. Rather, he has outlined what he sees as a helpful moral system that comes from these books. It is said of Jefferson that he would have joined the Unitarian Church had it existed in his era. He was in fact in dialogue with some of the forerunners in that tradition.

Jefferson concludes his section on religion in the *Notes to the State of Virginia* by suggesting that the shackles of religion must be removed before the citizens of that state could be fully free after the American Revolution. Virginia's Quakers, Presbyterians and Baptists joined with Jefferson to remove the privileges from the Anglican Church. Jefferson wrote the Statute in Virginia that finally established religious freedom in 1777 that read, "that no man shall be compelled to frequent or support any religious worship, place, or ministry whatsoever, nor shall be enforced, restrained, molested, or burthened in his body or goods, nor shall otherwise suffer on account of his religious opinions or belief" (Appleby, 2003. p. 59). When asked by some of his supporters to articulate his position, Jefferson is reported to have said, "I am for freedom of religion, and against all maneuvers to bring about a legal ascendancy of one sect over another" (Appleby, 2003. p. 60).

Jefferson's own theological position was very different from that of the Presbyterians, Baptists, or Quakers who were some of his allies. Yet, by drawing together all those religions that reflected the minority in their various colonies and subsequent states, he was able to win freedom of religion through the first amendment to the U.S. Constitution. There is a footnote in history that the First Amendment stated the Federal authority. However, in such states as those in New England, the Congregational tradition was able well into the nineteenth century to continue legal dominance (Appleby, 2003. p. 61). It is clear that from Jefferson's perspective the role of the First Amendment right of religious freedom was not an effort to protect the church from the corruption of civil government as found in the views of Roger Williams. Rather, it was directed at insuring that civil government is protected from the church.

Impact Today

Today the two concepts of freedom of religion and separation of church and state are seen as fundamentally one right that is based on the First Amendment to the U.S. Constitution. This difference was significant, however, to many persons in the eighteenth century. Persons in each colony and state who were considered to be the *dissenters* by the persons from the majority religions were clear that the First Amendment meant that they could worship in their own way. Thus, freedom of religion was clearly a benefit. Since freedom of religion is couched in this amendment with other freedoms, this is a reasonable conclusion. However, for persons from the majority who liked having their clergy paid by government taxes, the benefit of this new legislation was less clear.

Ironically it was this first issue which offered Thomas Jefferson opportunity to muddy the waters and include the separation of church and state to the implications of the First Amendment. In 1805 the Danbury Baptist Association was working to petition the Connecticut Legislature to bring freedom of religion into state laws. In an effort to gain support for their position, they called on then President Jefferson to offer an opinion. In his now famous letter to the Danbury Baptist Association, Jefferson assures them that the first amendment creates a firm wall of separation between church and state (Hamburger, 2002. p. 481). Since President Jefferson represented federal authority at this time, his letter had little impact on the Connecticut Legislature. However, these same issues came up again just after the Civil War. President Grant, in an effort to appeal to nativists, proposed a constitutional amendment that was intended to insure the clear separation of church and state. For this, he employed the Jeffersonian interpretation of the first amendment found in the letter to the Danbury Baptist Association as an authoritative source as to the intent of the first amendment. Today we live with the original myth created by Jefferson that the first amendment statement of freedom of religion also includes separation of church and state. "The First Amendment, that was written to limit government, has been interpreted directly to constrain religion" (Hamburger, 2002. p. 484).

Historically, there have always been those in religion who have attempted to have direct participation in activities of the state, while there are others who have avoided it. This distinction has not always been a matter of faith or belief, but rather a reflection of the practical realities of the congregation. Clergy and church councils have long avoided offending key members who reflect different opinions. Specifically, to take a position that a key benefactor would disagree with would be problematic.

Often at the fringes of this debate are two conflicting understandings of religious liberty. On the one hand, the traditional religious perspective of the nineteenth century theologian Alexis de Tocqueville and others was that the church did not need to dictate laws that reflected the views of the church. Rather, under the banner of morals, the church would persuade the general public into *right thinking* on various subjects. Even today, religion masquerades under the cloak of morality among politicians, most notably in the 1980s with the Moral Majority.

On the other side of this debate is the original Jeffersonian position that fears creeds, clergy, and anything else that will prevent individuals from thinking for themselves. Jefferson was concerned that outspoken clergy could persuade parishioners to vote as a group rather than from their own consciences. Clearly many Americans, including Thomas Jefferson, Andrew Jackson, theological liberals and others fear a strong clergy voice. This reflected for the first two centuries in the split between Catholics and Protestants. Ironically, however, today this split is more between Evangelicals and Liberals, both Protestant and Catholic.

The metaphor first offered by Williams and picked up by Jefferson of the *wall of separation* offers a simple interpretation of the basic principles that are held by most persons in the United States. Ironically, this concept is truly foreign to persons from European countries and to other former colonies, such as Australia. While most of these countries today practice freedom of religion, there is also no prohibition to supporting religion as seems appropriate. For example, in Australia, there is no problem funding a chaplain with government funds, if that chaplain offers a needed service for nursing home residents.

In elder services since World War II, this wall has also had an impact. In the 1950 and 1960 White House Conferences on Aging, there were sections on religion. However, by 1970, it was seen as problematic to have a section on religion due to the political interpretation of separation of church and state that was present at that time. Thus, in preparation for the 1970 White House Conference, Clark Tibbits, in conjunction with other White House Conference staff, came up with the concept of Spiritual Well-being. Popular at that time were psychological well-being or happiness scales. These scales measured how emotionally happy one was. It seemed reasonable to parallel this concept in terms of spiritual happiness. Arthur Flemming was in charge of the 1971 conference, and according to interviews conducted by James Ellor and Melvin Kimble prior to the death of Dr. Flemming, after Tibbits and his team developed the Spiritual Well-being concept, it was then field tested in Indiana by a group chaired by Grover Heartman. The feedback from this conference was good, so Paul Maves was asked to write the concept paper for the 1971 conference. In an interview conducted by Ellor and Kimble with Maves, he noted that he had written the 1961 White House Conference papers and was then asked to write the 1971 conference papers. However, he was in the process of moving to St. Paul School of Theology in Kansas City, and did not feel that he had the time. Thus, David O. Moberg was asked to write this paper. Thus, it is often thought that Dr. Moberg was the originator of the Spiritual Well-being concept. To politicians in the early 70s the concept of Spiritual Well-being was less offensive to the separation of church and state than the more common term, religion. By the 1984 White House Conference, both Spiritual Well-being and religion were considered offensive to the sensibilities of those in charge, so the paper for this conference was written on ethics, not dissimilar to the above discussion of morality as a smoke screen for religion.

The impact of the separation of church and state can also be seen in the Older American's Act. One of the congressional aides who worked on the wording of the original legislation was also a rabbinic scholar. He knew that in his synagogue there was a large room with a kitchen in it that would be a fit place to hold congregate dining. Thus, he suggested in the legislation that religious congregations are good places to put congregate dining sites. Reports from the various states over the years have suggested that the use of church basements was more common when the Older American's Act was new, than it is today. Many church, synagogue or temple basements do not meet the accessibility laws for handicapped persons as they often have steps, without elevators for access.

The White House Office for Faith-Based and Community Initiatives is clearly held in the spotlight of the separation of church and state. Ironically, this initiative seems to have been bombarded from both sides of the issue. On the one hand, the Jeffersonian liberals and dissenter traditions were concerned about this office because they wanted to protect those services already funded by government sources. The issue was articulated in terms of not wanting churches to be allowed to take contracts away from legitimate service providers. Another concern was raised that church based providers would want to reduce the educational requirements to provide such services as day care and even counseling. Numerous letters and speeches have been orated that pronounce the *evangelical right* as the enemy to other religions. Tactics reminiscent of the anti-Catholic movements of the eighteenth and nineteenth centuries have been mobilized to prevent such services as provided by congregations from gaining access to public funding for their services.

At the same time, the Roger Williams *religionists* view the prospect of public funding as giving too much control to government of the programs that they have worked to develop in their congregations. Fear of everything from too much paper work to the burden of too many public regulations would soil the sanctity of the church.

The battle for a useful definition of the first amendment's freedom of religion continues today with the vision that the amendment requires a wall of separation. Yet we live with the paradox that the United States Senate can have a chaplain for their members, our money can say *in God we trust*, the president can follow the lead of our Second President Thomas Jefferson by writing to various clergy groups and consulting with clergy on how to influence their followers to vote for him, and yet, we do not allow prayer in schools and we do not want congregations to receive public funding to provide social services.

Clearly the arguments intended to preserve the purity of the church as well as those who hope to save the public square from the influence of religion are alive and well in the current epoch. Possibly President Grant was correct when he attempted to clarify the First Amendment with a new amendment that granted both freedom of religion and the separation of church and state. The current White House Office for Faith-Based and Community Initiatives was conceived by then Governor Bush, who discovered in Texas that traditional services in the field of addictions were forcing faith-based providers out of business as they did not meet the standards of the public services. Yet, it was his feeling that they did a better job of treatment. This question regarding the actual impact of being faith-based is one that is still in contention.

The Pew Charitable Trusts, among others, have funded multiple initiatives designed to address the many questions surrounding the provision of services by faith-based organizations. Funding *The Roundtable on Religion and Social Welfare Policy* has begun the generation of numerous publications focusing on faith-based service provision. Of particular relevance to the questions surrounding church and state and freedom of religion is a joint effort by the Roundtable with The George Washington University Law School and Search for Common Ground–USA, in which George Washington Law School professors Ira C. Lupu and Robert W. Tuttle explore the current state of the law. However, the fundamental question as to the interpretation of the first amendment will remain in the hands of the Supreme Court unless a new amendment to the Constitution is successful some time in the future. And as Lupu and Tuttle point out, constitutional law is only the beginning in light of the complex interplay between the Establishment Clause of the First Amendment, recent cases in the courts, state constitutional law, the law of employment discrimination, federal programs that invite faith-based participation, and state social service contracts with faith-based organizations. Legal advocates and religious scholars will be examining these issues for years to come.

REFERENCES

Appleby, J. (2003). *Thomas Jefferson.* New York: Holt and Co.

Calvin, J. (1993). *Commentary on a Harmony of the Evangelists, Matthew, Mark, and Luke* (W. Pringle, Trans.). Grand Rapids: Baker Book House.

Hamburger, P. (2002). *Separation of Church and State.* Cambridge: Harvard University Press.

Hamilton, A., Madison, J., & Jay, J. (1961). *The Federalist Papers.* New York: Penguine Press.

Jefferson, T. (1982). *Notes on the State of Virginia.* Chapel Hill: The University of North Carolina Press.

Jefferson, T. (1989). *The Jefferson Bible.* Boston: Beacon Press.

Jensen, M. (1940). *The Articles of Confederation: An Interpretation of the Social-Constitutional History of the American Revolution.* Madison: The University of Wisconsin Press.

Lupu, I. C., & Tuttle, R. W. (2002). *Government Partnerships with Faith-Based Service Providers: The State of the Law.* Albany: Round Table Discussion on Religion and Social Policy.

Nelson, J. L. (2000). *All the Brave Fellows.* New York: Pocket Books.

Peterson, M. D. (Ed.). (1975). *The Portable Thomas Jefferson.* New York: A Penguin Book.

Micro Practice and Faith-Based Initiatives: The Role of Religious Congregations in the Social Service System

James W. Ellor, PhD

SUMMARY. Religious organizations have provided services for older adults for thousands of years. For the sons and daughters of Abraham, this is Biblically mandated. Charitable Choice and the President's Office of Faith-Based Initiatives is only the most recent effort to bring this informal caregiving system into dialogue with the remainder of the formal social service system in the United States. At this time, religious congregations play a gap-filling role in the community service system. Their services range from informal volunteer-driven approaches to a local need, to large formal service systems. From the first draft of the Older American's Act, nutrition sites have specifically named religious congregations in partners with the service system. Today this system continues to be ready to support at least the seniors in their own congregations. *[Article copies available for a fee from The Haworth Document Delivery Service: 1-800-HAWORTH. E-mail address: <docdelivery@haworthpress.com> Website: <http://www.HaworthPress.com> © 2004 by The Haworth Press, Inc. All rights reserved.]*

Rev. James W. Ellor is Director of the Institute of Gerontological Studies at Baylor University School of Social Work, Waco, TX 76798-7320. He is also Associate Director of the Center for Aging, Religion and Spirituality, St. Paul, MN (E-mail: James_Ellor@Baylor.Edu).

[Haworth co-indexing entry note]: "Micro Practice and Faith-Based Initiatives: The Role of Religious Congregations in the Social Service System." Ellor, James W. Co-published simultaneously in *Journal of Religious Gerontology* (The Haworth Pastoral Press, an imprint of The Haworth Press, Inc.) Vol. 16, No. 1/2, 2004, pp. 15-35; and: *Faith-Based Initiatives and Aging Services* (ed: F. Ellen Netting, and James W. Ellor) The Haworth Pastoral Press, an imprint of The Haworth Press, Inc., 2004, pp. 15-35. Single or multiple copies of this article are available for a fee from The Haworth Document Delivery Service [1-800-HAWORTH, 9:00 a.m. - 5:00 p.m. (EST). E-mail address: docdelivery@haworthpress.com].

http://www.haworthpress.com/web/JRG
© 2004 by The Haworth Press, Inc. All rights reserved.
Digital Object Identifier: 10.1300/J078v16n01_02

15

KEYWORDS. Religious congregations, Faith-Based Initiatives, social services, aging, Charitable Choice

INTRODUCTION

Beginning with Charitable Choice legislation, followed by the development of the Office of Faith-Based and Community Initiatives, there has been an on-going public discourse about the implications and challenges for social service delivery at the local level. The aged are not a primary target of either the Office of Faith-Based and Community Initiatives, of Charitable Choice or of subsequent efforts to incorporate faith-based organizations into the mainstream of social service delivery. However, these efforts clearly have implications for social service practice, which subsequently have implications for seniors. Simultaneously, the presence of faith-based initiatives evokes the need to better understand the nature of faith-based organizations as they address the needs of older adults. This chapter will explore the nature of faith-based services, their role in the community service system and their impact on micro or direct practice.

THE CONTEXT OF SOCIAL SERVICES

Within the past twenty-five years since Ronald Reagan first began to publicly suggest that religious congregations should play a more active role in the social service community (Thornburgh & Wolfer, 2000), many aspects of service delivery have changed. In 1980, the Older American's Act was reaching maturity, becoming an established part of the formula for social service funding. The Vietnam War was over and the country was rethinking how government is to respond to citizen needs under the new Republican leadership. In this context, there was a great deal of concern that the Reagan administration simply wanted religious congregations to replace paid social services in support of older adults. Although this change did not come to pass, it did launch the first round of research and study as to the role of religious congregations in social services to older adults.

Today five forces have converged to alter the way community-based services for older adults are provided: (1) amendments to (and changing allocations in) the Older American's Act; (2) the Personal Responsibility and Work Opportunity Reconciliation Act of 1996 (PRWORA)

(P.L. 104-193) which initiated Charitable Choice; (3) the general economic struggle in the United States with its implications for charitable giving; (4) the deep concern around terrorism and the attacks of September 11, 2001; and (5) the wars in Afghanistan and Iraq (Dudley, 2002, p. 10.) Each of these forces have impacted the shape of services through funding, volunteerism, and the general climate for neighborhood response to human need.

Since its inception, The Older American's Act has been an important force in assuring the availability of social services for older adults at the local level. Interestingly, within this discussion of faith-based initiatives, the Older American's Act contains some of the earliest language as to one role played by religious congregations in government funded social services. According to Byron Gold, a congressman's aide who was working on drafting the original Older American's Act, when it came to discussions of nutrition sites for older adults, as a Rabbinic Scholar, he knew that his synagogue had a large room in the basement with a kitchen at one end. He also knew that this was common in many synagogues and churches in the United States. Thus, there is language suggesting this sort of site in the Older American's Act. Hosting such activities is only one way in which congregations can serve the needs of seniors; however, it is significant that the Older American's Act led the way in recognizing this valuable resource in the community.

The Personal Responsibility and Work Opportunity Reconciliation Act of 1996 (PRWORA) (P.L. 104-193), commonly referred to as the "Welfare to Work" law, offers incentives for various state agencies to work with current welfare recipients to become self-sufficient. It further implements termination dates for public assistance. Due to this transition in how the nation takes care of persons in poverty, shifts in funding have diverted monies from traditional "welfare" providers to offer job assistance, employment training, and vocational counseling programs.

This legislation is of less direct importance to older adults than it would be to younger families. However, to the extent that younger families depend on having a grandparent living with them, in order to have his or her social security check supplement the family income, then it matters. It will also matter for the future, when persons affected by these changes become older themselves. However, it may be that the larger potential impact is on the nature and structure of social agencies and how they do their work. The traditional "welfare system" is being replaced by employment and educational services and the emphasis is now on self-sufficiency. With the initiation of this 1996 legislation, the economy was booming and jobs were available. After 9/11/2001, this is no longer the case. Historically it has been faith-based services and con-gregations that have become the gap-filling services between "welfare and work." Individuals requesting short-term assistance, clothing and food from pantries and other services are the gap fillers, at least for younger populations.

The third force has been a general downturn in personal charity and corporate philanthropy. Donations to non-profit agencies, faith-based ministries and other charitable services has gone down since 9/11 (Dudley, 2002, p. 10.) In part due to the slowing of the general economy and in part a reflection of changes in tax laws, there seems to be less money coming in to support the various services for older adults. Unfor-tunately, the downturn in giving coincides with the increased needs in many communities.

The deepening concern around terrorism has had a mixed impact on social services. On the one hand, it has made some communities more suspicious of one another and thus, inhibited cooperation. However, in other communities, it has brought a new spirit of working together to solve community problems, which includes a wider variety of faith-based congregations, including mosques.

Finally, the wars in Afghanistan and Iraq have reduced the amount of public money in general available for social services. To date this has had a somewhat reduced impact on Older American's Act services in terms of budget reductions, but in other areas of social service, it has slowed the growth to below the rate of inflation. In the post Iraq war time frame, it is clear that discretionary funding for all social services is in danger of dwindling.

The critical theme, given these political-economic forces, is the shrinking dollar for the support of social services for older adults. Since the inception of the Office of Faith-Based and Community Initiatives, the great fear of the social service sector has been that there would be a deliberate attempt on the part of the Federal Government to replace paid professional social service providers with voluntary faith-based ser-vices. Concerns have been expressed about the professional preparation of faith-based workers as well as the nature of the services themselves. In our interviews with representatives of the Office of Faith-Based and Community Initiatives, we understood them to say that all of the "stan-dards" in the rules and laws were to be upheld. The faith-based initia-tives were aimed at expanding those eligible to receive government funds to provide services, not to alter the quality of the services. How-ever, clearly fears persist.

As of the writing of this article, the predicted cuts in social service funds have taken root. As dollars shift over to defense and homeland security, social services in this country have fewer dollars to spend. However, fewer dollars for services does not equate into having fewer clients with needs. With the baby boom about to reach Golden Pond, the needs for services will predictably be increasing, while the public dollars for services will be shrinking. Historically, when this happens, the social service system turns to the voluntary sector for help.

Identifying a Faith-Based Service

Faith-based services are as diverse as any other group of social services in the community. They range from primarily informal congregationally based supportive responses to human need, to formal social service agencies. At the higher end of this continuum, there is a large group of faith-based agencies who have always been affiliated in one way or another to one of the major denominations. Such groups as the Salvation Army, Catholic Charities, Lutheran Social Services, and The Jewish Federation to name a few, have an identity with a particular religious tradition; however, since most of them have accepted public funding since the 1960s, they operate like most other public or non-sectarian services in the community. Indeed in some cases, there is a constant dialogue as to what it truly means to continue to identify with that denomination, since they accept persons from all traditions and non-traditions as clients. The article in this volume by F. Ellen Netting directly addresses the issues for these groups.

Other agencies in the community can trace their roots to a particular denomination or congregation, but have been "spun off" by that group and are now operated by social workers and other professionals outside of the religious community. One of the common patterns of faith-based services is that they are created by a congregation, or local group or denomination at a time when this agency fills a gap in community services. However, as the agency grows, it is "spun" off from the host organization, obtaining its own corporation status and progressively moving to become more independent of the original congregation or denomination of origin. These groups, like the first, have been competing for and working with public funding for many years.

Possibly the more unique level of faith-based initiatives are those found in congregations. These groups have long confused formal service providers, since they may range from a strictly informal relationship within the congregation to a more formal type of structured association. One very common scenario can be seen when Mrs. Smith needs a ride to the doctor. She calls her church where the phone is answered by a secretary. The secretary may or may not check with the pastor, but eventually links Mrs. Smith up with Mr. Jones who gives her a ride to the doctor. There is no case record kept, and no means test applied. Whether or not Mrs Smith gets the ride is often a subjective evaluation by either a minister, priest or Rabbi who determines if Mrs. Smith really has a need, or if she is just fighting with her daughter, and her daughter should really provide the transport. In these cases occasional needs are generally responded to with some enthusiasm. However, like any other informal system, volume is the enemy to service provision. This sort of system works well when Mrs. Smith and a few other people have a problem. However, if 100 people started to call the office, the congregation would need a different response. In these cases, either all requests end up denied, or the congregation will initiate a more formal procedure.

An example of this was observed in one suburban community where several times a week the various congregations received persons who dropped by in need of food. All of the six congregations in the community gave out coupons from a local grocery store for this sort of need. With the recent "Welfare to Work" legislation, the congregations began seeing an increase in the complexity of needs. For example, homeless persons had multiple needs, whereas previous service recipients had just needed a little help to get by. One of the congregations hired a minister who was also a social worker. As he saw this unraveling situation, he began to talk to the other congregations and they also then began to compare notes. Two of the congregations had begun to keep records by name and address of any persons who stopped by for this sort of assistance who were not members of their congregations. It seemed that one of the congregations when confronted with this same scenario gave out $40 in grocery coupons while the other gave out $60. However, the more generous congregation would run out of budget around September, at which point the first congregation clearly began to receive more persons who were coming over to them from the second one.

When the six congregations began to compare notes, there was clearly a group that they were all seeing, often in the same week. Each one professed to belong to the denomination in which they were standing at the time. Many of them could also be traced for over a two-year period for which records were kept. The social worker then asked the question, is this really the best way to help people in need? The congregations were feeling ripped off by this group of people, which meant that one had abruptly stopped helping them. The other congregations were confused as to how to help. There was, however, a formal social service agency in the community that had been developed years ago to help such persons. The group determined that they would use their church buses to transport persons who did not have a car to this agency, rather than giving out grocery coupons. They also then turned their budgets for this sort of giving over to that agency. With the initiation of this new policy, the number of requests greatly dropped off and those that did seek assistance at the agency seemed to find new options for meeting their needs.

Some of the activities of these informal helpers may not be appropriate, other activities are vital for the community. In either case, however, it often takes social services working together with congregations to offer appropriate support systems. Since 1980 there have been several initiatives from public and private sources to try to create formal linkages between congregations and social services. Some have been more successful than others.

Range of Service Providers

In order to make sense out of the pattern of both formal and informal services, Tobin et al. (1986) based on their research on the role of churches, synagogues, temples and mosques in the community service system developed the following categories of services found in congregations. Congregations do not clearly fit into any one of these categories since they will often provide different services in different contexts for different populations. For example, it is not unusual for a congregation to either have developed or to be hosting a day care center for children, and yet, provide only occasional pastoral support for seniors on an informal basis. The categories that this study surfaced are: (1) Providing Religious Services; (2) Providing Pastoral Services; (3) the Church as Host; and (4) the Church as Service Provider.

Providing Religious Services: Congregations have as their primary task the provision of religious services to their membership. These services are often very important to the members, both for spiritual nurture as well as for emotional well-being. Religious services can include everything from formal worship, to the study of religious literature, to clubs or small groups that offer fellowship with other persons from the congregation.

Providing Pastoral Services: Generally provided by clergy or a trained layperson, pastoral services can range from a simple visit during an illness, to intense counseling at a time of crisis. This role often also includes some service provision. If a parishioner is in crisis and needs some food, congregations often give a gift certificate for a local grocery store, or even a bag of groceries.

The Church as Host: Particularly since the inclusion of religious congregations in the Older American's Act, there have been social services who rent space in religious congregations. Often much of the space in a church, synagogue, or temple is unused during the week. Day care centers, nutrition sites, and even counseling services can be found in that space that is then turned over to the church on the weekend for religious activities. In this category, there is generally little or no contact between the worshiping congregation and the providers and recipients of the social services. The service just rents space.

The Church as Service Provider: Some religious congregations actually provide direct social services to older adults in the community. Funded and fully supported by the congregation, these services are often modest in size and scope, but robust in the intention of offering quality services to their community. Traditionally, such services are developed in religious congregations, but eventually they are "spun off" of the congregation at the point at which they become self-sufficient and able to carry on under their own corporation.

These four roles reflect some of the differences between the informal and the formal, yet they can all be provided by the same congregation, thus failing to place the individual church, synagogue, temple, or mosque on a single axis. Rather than referring to religious congregations as representing a single role on this continuum, it can be suggested that they play a more fluid role moving between the two extremes depending on factors that are not generally based upon the religious congregation's desire to necessarily become a formal service provider. The clearest predictor in the research as to what types of congregations are providing which services is reflective of the sensitivity to the needs of older adults who are within the congregation. This sensitivity goes beyond the clergy or the various decision-making boards within the congregation. Numerous examples of sensitive clergy that can't get programs past the church board or vice versa can be found. There are clearly three groups that must be sensitive: (1) The clergy, since they are frequently the gate keepers for programs; (2) the boards, and (3) the elders themselves. A lot of good programs die in religious congregations due to a lack of lay leadership, or a lack of support from the elderly members.

Uniqueness of Faith-Based Services

Clearly, one of the ways inter-faith caregivers are different from many social service agencies in the formal system is their wholistic philosophy. The concept of Wholism is not new. Adler talks of taking a holistic view of the needs of clients as early as the 1920s. More recently, Granger Westberg brought forth the concept of the "Wholistic" approach to meeting health needs. While many different authors have conceptualized this philosophy differently, they have one thing in common. All of the authors discuss the nature of the person as having several different aspects or dimensions. These include the emotional self, the physical self, the social self, and the "fourth dimension" or the spiritual self added by Granger Westberg.

Each of the four dimensions can be conceptualized as separate entities. The psychologist can address the emotions, the recreation therapist can deal with the social, the physician can heal the body, and the clergy person can minister to the soul. The important contribution of Alfred Adler was to point out that it is difficult to try to address each of these dimensions as if the others did not exist. The concept of wholism advocates the inclusion of all four dimensions in any assessment or treatment approach.

While the inclusion of all four dimensions is important, the functional question for persons providing services is, "How do we integrate the various aspects of the person into service?" The social worker or clergy person is not a physician or nurse. Thus, they are often reluctant to delve too far into the medical needs of seniors. The need is for sensitivity in identifying needs and the ability to appropriately refer to persons who specialize in areas with which the practitioner is not as familiar.

Possibly the most difficult question when attempting to discuss a wholistic philosophy is the nature of the integration of the various aspects of the person. How do the four dimensions fit together? A review of the literature suggests that there are three different views regarding the integration of the four dimensions (Eller, 1983, p. 26). Most often the four are simply perceived as separate. Much like four pieces of a pie, they can be separated and addressed one at a time. A service that would reflect such a philosophy might be a medical clinic in which if the individual needed medical care he or she would see a physician. If he or she needed emotional counseling, he or she would move down the hall to the psychologist or social worker, and the same for a chaplain or recreation therapist. The clinic could claim to be wholistic because all the needed services were available. Yet, in this model the burden for integration is on the patient.

A second perspective suggests that one of the dimensions is foundational to the other three. Thus, for example, the medical community might argue that without the physical, the other three would not exist. Therefore, the foundation of the person is his or her physical self. To operationalize this philosophy, an agency might hire physicians or nurses to do all of the services from counseling to prayer.

The final perspective would argue that one of the various aspects of the person provides an integrative force for the person, permeating all others. Thus, the focal dimension could not be separated from the other three, but rather provides the glue that integrates and holds together the other aspects of the person. Thus a service might see the emotional aspect to be the integrative force. If this is the case, the counselor would work to facilitate intellectual and emotional integration with the client.

The National Interfaith Coalition summarizes one opinion on the spiritual, that reflects this final perspective, when they state, "The Spiritual is not one dimension among many in life; rather, it permeates and gives meaning to all life" (National Interfaith Coalition on Aging, 1980). A wholistic philosophy would acknowledge and attempt to address the needs of all four aspects of the person, yet it would understand that it is the spiritual dimension that holds the individual together, providing an integrative force in the lives of people. This means that wholistic agencies would not only need to address the spiritual needs of clients, in the sense of giving them rides to worship, but rather, it would mean interacting with the client, facilitating the articulation and insight into the nature of the spirit, and the role of the spiritual in helping to integrate life.

Today the language of a wholistic philosophy has been challenged by the term, Spiritual. Many formerly wholistic agencies now suggest that their commonality is in their approach to the spiritual needs of clients. This term is clear for some religious traditions, and less clear for others. It is clear for Roman Catholic and Jewish mystical traditions as well as persons from Buddhist and Hindu traditions. It is less a part of the nomenclature for many protestant groups who understand and use terms such as soul or God's spirit, but not spiritual in reference to a person. Historically, the term religion when applied dogmatically, has made it harder to bring together congregations and denominations to work together in social services, since there are many age old reasons for the separation of the various groups. Therefore, for many Protestants who may not have previously used the term, spirituality has taken over from wholism to be a bonding concept. Spirituality in this case is used to reflect a personal, rather than congregate or corporate, relationship with the Divine (God) or creation depending on the definition of the individual using the term. In this sense, each person understands something slightly different about its meaning. Yet, it seems to be the term that bonds together the various efforts to view the person as more than physical, social or emotional elements.

It is within this context of language and the use of spirituality (previously wholism) that many congregations are ministering to older adults. Congregational practice is becoming more and more a part of the micro practice delivery system.

Congregations and Aging Ministries

As stated earlier, the concept of faith-based social services is not new (see Ellor, 1996). When the Office of Faith-Based Initiatives came into being, one of the concerns was that faith-based service providers like Catholic Charities, the Salvation Army, Lutheran Social Services, and the Jewish Federation were already very much a part of the community social service network and were already receiving governmental funding. The new players in this thrust are not the major social service agencies who are founded and often continue to be funded by congregations and denominations. Rather, it is the smaller agencies and congregations that reflect a new constituency for this office. Congregations and the smaller agencies that have often sprung from them are often misunderstood by the formal social service sector. In this chapter, the focus is on the role of the religious congregation in providing social services within the aging network.

Studies of the social services provided by religious congregations have demonstrated the presence of services for many years. The earliest studies by Cook (Cook, 1976) and Steinitz (Steinitz, 1981) and subsequent studies by Tobin, Ellor (Tobin et al., 1986), and Fahey identified numerous ways that local congregations are involved in serving older adults. The services found in faith-based congregations of all denominations are difficult to categorize. They range from grasping tightly to the designation of a voluntary, informal, service primarily to their own members, to the more formalized services to the community at large. Studies by Veroff and Kulka (1981) suggest that families are first turned to by elders in times of a crisis. Studies of family caregiving suggest that 70-80 percent of all of the needs of the elders are provided for by members of the immediate family. Clearly, the family unit is the principle caregiver for the needs of any person who is physically or emotionally impaired. Beyond the family unit, there is a continuum of services that range from the informal to the formal that provide support. At the informal end of this continuum, Froland and Pancoast (Froland & Pancoast, 1981, p. 46) suggested that there are six categories of informal helpers. These are: family and friends; neighbors; natural helpers; role related helpers; people with similar problems and volunteers.

INFORMAL HELPERS

Family and Friends: First, elders turn to friends and families in times of need. Often friends and informal helpers such as religious congregations are turned to sooner by seniors whose family does not live in the area. However, even when family members are available, seniors and families turn to their minister, priest or rabbi very quickly for support. In many ways, it is considered more acceptable to visit a clergy person in a time of need, particularly if the problem seems to reflect emotional or cognitive dysfunction. This is particularly true for the cohort that is now in the oldest old, or 85+ age group.

Neighbors: When seniors live in an area where they know their neighbors and have found mutual support systems with them, the person next door is often both able and willing to help out in times of significant need. Therefore, neighbors become a resource when family members may not be as accessible.

Natural Helpers: Every community has a few individuals who simply seem to show up in times when someone in their area has a problem or significant need. Known as natural helpers, several studies have tried to find ways for formal social services to identify and harness this group to obtain assistance in times of need, but most efforts have been unsuccessful. Natural helpers assist out of the goodness of their hearts, often not reflecting a need for recognition or formal role definition.

Role Related Helpers: This group reflects individuals whose primary employment brings them into contact with older adults, but whose job description is not primarily in the social services. For example, postal workers are employed to deliver the mail. However, particularly mail carriers with walking routes notice things about the patrons along the way. If there is a senior who is always there to greet him or her at the door, but then suddenly for several days is not present, and the house seems to be unattended, there are now phone numbers for the letter carries to call and this will send a police office and often a social worker out to the home, just to be sure the senior has not fallen and is unable to call for help. In the same way, some grocery stores may not have a home delivery service, but if a senior calls and there is time, maybe a stocker can be employed to carry the groceries over to the home of the senior. Clergy are generally considered to be role related helpers as well. Their primary job description is to serve the congregation, but not necessarily the entire community. Their job also often includes administration, preaching, teaching and other functions performed for the congregation that are not reflected in the job description of a social worker.

People with Similar Problems: This category is intended to identify persons with the same disease, or emotional problem, such as a depression support group, or group for persons with cancer. Among older adults, senior centers, senior clubs and other places where elders congregate provide this sort of service. These services are often less geographically bound than are the other types of informal service providers. They can be national groups such as the National Council on the Aged or the American Association of Retired Persons, but they can also reflect local chapters that are tied to national bodies.

Volunteers: The final group of informal service providers are volunteers. Volunteers serve both public and private social service agencies. One can also call the deacons in a church or the health cabinet in a synagogue volunteers in a faith-based congregation. Often when funds are being cut by government, local social service agencies will call upon local congregations to help provide volunteers to fill in for staff lost in budget cuts. Unfortunately, in many instances, when this happens, they are competing for a scarce resource, as many congregations these days have a difficult time finding volunteers to do all the committee work and meeting and greeting that is found in the life of a local parish.

As noted, clergy fit into this concept as "Role Related Helpers." Role Related Helpers are persons who are in positions to help older adults; however, their primary job descriptions are not necessarily as a service provider to older adults. Other role related helpers are postal workers, store keepers, and pharmacists. The work of Froland and Pancoast provide insight as to how clergy fit into the aging network. However, the work of Steinitz (1981) would suggest that more than 80 percent of the actual services provided by churches and synagogues for older adults are provided by lay persons, not clergy. Thus, it is helpful to know how clergy fit into the "aging network," but it would be naive to assume that this image provides the whole picture.

Examination of the role of the religious congregation, when there is sensitivity to the needs of older adults, suggest that congregations play a bridging role between the informal and the formal. They have access to the best of both worlds. On the other hand, there is always the darker side. When there is a lack of sensitivity, some religious congregations play a more negative role that frustrates the formal network, and frequently, albeit accidentally, participates in ageism, or gerontophobia. Clearly the task of those of us who are sensitive to the role that the religious congregation can play in the lives of elders is to facilitate the movement from darkness into light.

FORMAL AND INFORMAL PROVIDERS WORKING TOGETHER

Efforts funded by national foundations over the past twenty years have focused on drawing religious congregations into communication and interaction with social service agencies to serve the needs of older adults. The Robert Wood Johnson Foundation through its Interfaith Caregivers Initiative and the Retirement Research Foundation through its Congregational Connection Program have developed two models for service provision.

The Interfaith Caregivers approach reflected communities of congregations working together to provide services. One model employed by this group reflected a division of needs among a group of congregations. For example, one congregation addresses meals, another provides transportation, and still another facilitates fellowship. Together the three congregations provide for the needs of the community elders.

The approaches developed by the Retirement Research Foundation's Congregational Connection program were developed originally by soliciting denominations in the Chicago area to submit a proposal. The denomination that was awarded funding then received training in older adult ministries for their congregations. Finally, individual congregations were supported to develop specific ministries for their communities. The most recent generation of this model involves congregations working with a social service mentor to develop programs and services to seniors. Both groups offer viable models for developing social services. Like any such initiative, some of the congregations continue many years later to provide services and expand programming while others have not survived.

Tobin, Ellor and Anderson-Ray (Tobin et al., 1986, p. 148) suggested in their studies of communities of congregations that there seemed to be some sense that to work with a local social service or even another agency would mean loss of control and particularly if there was government funding involved, a lost of congregational values. The Office of Faith-Based and Community Initiatives has worked to try to insure that congregations do not have to give up their identities as religious organizations in order to host social services. However, such services do need to comply with current federal standards.

The second concern that Tobin, Ellor, and Anderson-Ray found was that congregations thought that the only way to work together was to do so in complete collaboration, where the two groups stood the chance of losing their separate identities. In their book, *Enabling the Elderly*, the authors note that there are actually five levels of interaction possible. It is more of a continuum of possibilities. The five levels offered are "communication," "cooperation," "coordination," "collaboration," and "confederation" (Tobin et al., 1986, p. 1248). Each is described below.

Communication simply involves dialogue and other forms of information sharing between agencies. In a community where none of the agencies or congregations talk with one another, a simple meeting to inform others about one's services or concerns is communication. *Cooperation* moves to the next level as cooperation involves implementing independent programs, but working toward similar ends, therefore dialogue takes place to share information and work to eliminate any duplication of services. *Coordination* takes place when the two or more groups actually sit down and work to be sure that the services each provides separately can enhance each other. In this case each group maintains their own identity, and resources, yet each service is more complete by being engaged with the other. *Collaboration* is found in services or congregations that maintain their own identity, yet fully share resources. In this case it is not two services working together, but rather two agencies or congregations providing for one program. Finally, *confederation* takes place when the two congregations or agencies simply merge, creating a single host agency.

If a congregation and social service provider wish to work together, based on this continuum, when they first begin, most will start with simple communication. Thus, the support group at the church is advertised at the social service agency and the transportation program is advertised in the congregation. If there has never been any sort of communication in the past, this is an enviable place to be. The congregation does not need to feel as if, if they are not collaborating, they are somehow not involved. Communication is good. On the other hand, if they are already coordinating services, they may wish to stop having two independent caregiver support groups and hold one that is fed by resources out of both the congregation and the social service. This would allow them to move to a collaborative posture.

In actuality, the challenges of working together to serve the needs of old adults are more complicated than just the determination of what level of interaction is necessary. Like any endeavor, it reflects a complex process. Developing a service for older adults requires each group to understand each other. One variable reflects the unique role of religious professionals in congregations. Unlike the executive director of a social service agency, religious professionals (e.g., minister, rabbi, priest) play roles that may or may not legally reflect that of a chief executive and generally have other levels of authority that need to be addressed before final decisions can be made. Dynamically, for example in most Christian congregations, while the minister or priest has to have a hand in or approve the development of a new program or service for the aged, most of the time, it is actually developed by an energized lay person. Thus, an agency wishing to work with a congregation needs to start with the clergy, but would need to find a lay person from the congregation who wants to work with them on it. Many other things in some congregations are "top down," in terms of clergy involvement, but not the development of services. These types of services are as often initiated by a lay person as by a pastor. For many in the social services community this makes no sense. However, it is reflective of the formal/informal nature of religious congregations, many of which are not incorporated entities and thus do not have to conform to any designated structure. For nonprofit and governmental entities that are subject to the nuances of corporate status and/or mandated structures, accessing the structure of a congregation can be rather unsettling.

For the most part, religious congregations that provide services do so because they see a need. In this way, they are gap-filling organizations. Congregations see a need that has not been addressed, and then attempt to fill that need or gap, by providing something. Often such services start out by simply meeting the needs of a single parishioner. One family comes to the pastor or lay leader with a problem, and they find a solution. When the leadership recognizes that there are a number of people who have that particular need, then they begin to create some sort of group or institutional response. As the program or service becomes more expensive and in need of guidance by a social service professional, then there is often an effort to spin off the service, so that it can be more independent and receive financial support from a broader community base.

Working Together

Numerous arguments can be made for working together between congregations and social service agencies. Clearly, as in the example above, coordinated services have some advantages to both the congregation and the agency. However, too often, when congregations feel as if they have been taken advantage of by a particular population they simply stop serving them. Thus, services that might have been productive with some guidance from a social service professional are lost without a trace in the community. When agencies and congregations do work together, there is often a strength in the combination of the formal and informal providers. For example, a congregation may have more flexibility that allows it to do certain things that a provider agency may have to go to great lengths to do.

Barriers for Working Together

Some barriers are noteworthy to this type of collaboration. One barrier is the bias that anything that is done by the informal service system is somehow inferior to the formal system. When this attitude is present in social service agencies, it is too often projected to the pastor or lay leader. Congregation members may not see themselves as professionals in social service, but they are also not willing to be treated as servants by community agency staff. Social service professionals are often surprised by the number of ministers, priests and rabbis who have legitimate social service credentials, even at the doctoral level.

A second common barrier which has recently become even more of a problem is in communication. It has been observed by Tobin et al. (1986) that when there is a patient in a mental health clinic, if that patient is a member of a local congregation, his or her pastor is often a family therapist to the patient's family. This should mean that where both the pastor and family are willing, the pastor should be a part of the treatment team, at least in terms of discharge. Yet, numerous barriers now exist to any sort of communication between these two groups, particularly in light of privacy laws that will not allow hospitals to notify congregations when one of their members is in their facility.

Finally, there is a series of barriers within congregations for developing programs or services. First and foremost is a lack of lay persons willing to work on a given project. Clergy and even lay leadership may see the need, but if there isn't a lay person willing to take up the project, then it won't happen. Indeed, the sequence is often just the reverse. A lay person sees the need, and brings it to the pastor and/or lay leadership and then becomes the person in charge of that program. A perceived lack of expertise is another barrier, and finally a lack of financial resources is also important in thwarting this sort of endeavor.

Advocacy

One of the important roles of local congregations is to advocate for the needs of parishioners and members of their community. Clearly, this function is more or less effective depending on the situation and persons involved. However, clergy are involved at all levels of advocacy. According to Ellor and Coates (1985) there are three levels of advocacy: (1) case, (2) community, and (3) class advocacy. In case advocacy, the pastor or lay person sees a parishioner or community member having a problem that may be unaddressed, or not addressed appropriately, and try to intervene. For example, too often when seniors present in an emergency room, if they are confused and disoriented, it is assumed this is a chronic condition. If the pastor, however, knows this is not true, he or she needs to say something to the staff in order to correct this perception. In other cases where a person may need an advocate, clergy and lay leaders will at times be the logical support persons, particularly is the elder if known to them.

When clergy or lay leaders begin to notice that there are a number of persons with a particular need, this is where community advocacy starts. Congregations can come together to advocate for a solution, or even form a group to address it themselves. Finally, there are times when congregations and clergy become so involved in a particular issue that they take it up with state and federal governmental agencies. This is class advocacy, often called cause advocacy. It is designed to meet the needs of a particular class of persons using the definition of that term from sociology that simply means that a class is a group of people with some need in common, not necessarily reflecting on socio-economic status.

In many ways congregations are in very good positions to advocate for individuals. By knowing people where they live and often working with them for many years, clergy and lay advocates can and do play advocacy roles. Not all social agencies are receptive to clergy advocates. Yet, particularly when there isn't a family member available, faith-based individuals often fill a very real gap in this area.

Role of Faith-Based Services in the Community of Social Services for the Aged

Faith-based services play a number of roles in the community. In general, congregations play the role of *gap filling* agencies. This means that when a gap is identified in the local social service network, congregations will initiate such a service. Three types of *gap* can be identified. First is a *gap of adequacy*. This means that there may be meals-on-wheels available in the community; however, if there is a lengthy waiting list, such as the community that recently recorded a two-year waiting list for such services, there is a gap in terms of providing an adequate amount of services. This is often a difficult *gap* for clergy to identify if they end their investigation at the phone book and find the name of the local service. It requires further inquiry to find out that the waiting list is simply too long for this service to be considered to be adequate in the community.

The second type of *gap* is when there simply is not a given service within the community. Often congregations are involved in innovation in *gap* filling. For example, one church has a *mother's day out* program to assist young families with occasional needs for baby sitting during day time shopping trips. This same congregation found that caregivers of persons with Alzheimer's Disease have a similar need, so they initiated *caregiver's day out* for older adults. Thus, the gap may not have been originally identified in the early versions of the Older Americans' Act, but is clearly a need found in today's environment.

Finally, there may be a *philosophical gap* in services. This occurs when a congregation feels that something like a senior's day care center should be made available for persons who practice their own faith tradition, so that seniors can come together with others who share their own religion. Like parochial schools for children, this sort of gap is identified by a value system, rather than a pure needs-based criteria.

Religious congregations are often very creative in the formation of social service activities; however, historically, once the program has been launched, it is eventually *spun off*. In other words, as it is passed from being run by lay volunteers from a specific congregation or a group of congregations, to being run by professional social service workers, the congregation/s will then wish to move it to a more independent status by becoming their own 501(c)3 nonprofit agency. Eventually, they may even begin to charge rent for space or encourage the agency to move to their own quarters.

For clergy the picture is somewhat less clear. Many clergy play the *role related helper* as identified by Froland and Pancoast (1981). This means that as caring professionals who work in the community they are often sought out by both members of their congregation and others for various types of emotional, social and financial assistance. Some clergy are well trained for this role, others are not prepared at all to provide this sort of assistance. Clergy almost universally have other things to do beyond providing this sort of assistance. Thus, they often play *gate keeping* and *referral* roles for help seekers. Even clergy who are well trained for counseling, for example, find that as a pastor, he or she will play multiple roles in the lives of parishioners. There may well be role conflict between preaching a sermon and providing one-to-one counseling services, for example. Thus, a referral may be the best course of action. When agencies approach congregations for assistance, clergy often play *gate keeping* roles in that they will want to be involved initially in the dialogue; however, the people who generally provide the *real* services are going to be lay persons. At times this is frustrating for agency staff, as they may know that they need to talk with a given lay person, but somehow seem to need to stop off the path with the pastor, rather than going directly to the layperson who they know will be the one involved. Clergy are as different in these roles as they are in personality type and denomination affiliation. Each person will have his or her own preferences and approaches. For persons in social service agencies, the best approach is to talk with the clergy persons and try to listen to his or her concerns.

CONCLUSION

The landscape for social services offered in the community for older adults has changed since the original writing of the Older American's Act. The financial picture has changed with the economy and priorities of federal, state and local governmental officials. While programs for older adults are generally better funded than those of other age groups, there continue to be vast unmet needs. Congregations employing volunteers rather than paid staff for programs find that it is often a challenge to find a qualified volunteer to provide good services. Often congregational services that are built on one key volunteer find that when this person leaves or moves on, the program dies for lack of leadership. Congregations themselves provide a wide range of services of a *gap* filling nature. Clergy are involved at various levels, some providing services, some gate keeping, and others even obstructing services. Like any other informal service provider, congregations tend not to be able to handle large volumes of service needs without turning their efforts into a formal service program or spinning the program off to become independent. In this changing landscape of services, questions as to the nature of the religious or wholistic or spiritual identity of any given social service may be at question. It seems clearer when the agency is directly a part of the life of a congregation. However, it is less clear once the program has moved off site and become independent. Thus, the current discourse regarding what a faith-based service really looks like from a micro perspective is ripe with questions. Is it simply a smaller agency with roots in a faith tradition? Or, is there more to it? This too will vary by program and community. In short, the nature of community faith-based services reflects a wide variety of priorities, needs, and resources offered by complex voluntary agencies for which the human needs of the community are only one priority in a larger landscape of congregational agendas.

REFERENCES

Cook, T. C. (1976). *The Religious Sector Explores Its Mission in Aging*. Athens: National Interfaith Coalition on Aging.

Dudley, C. S. (2002). *Community Ministry: New Challenges, Proven Steps to Faith-Based Initiatives*. Bethesda: Alban Institute.

Ellor, J. W. & R. B. Coates (1985). Examining the Role of the Church and Aging. *Journal of Religion and Aging* 2(1).

Ellor, J., E., E. Netting, & J. Thibault (1999). *Understanding Religious and Spiritual Aspects of Human Service Practice*. Columbia: The University of South Carolina Press.

Froland, C., D. L. Pancoast, N.J. Chapman, & P. J. Kimboko. (1981). *Helping Networks and Human Services*. Beverly Hills: Sage Publications.

Huber, L. W. (1995). The Church in the Community. *In Aging, Spirituality, and Religion*. M. Kimble, S. McFadden, J. Ellor, & J. Seeber (Eds.). Minneapolis, Fortress Press: 285-305.

Steinitz, L. Y. (1981). The local church as support for the elderly. *Journal of Gerontological Social Work* 4(1): 43-53.

Thornburgh, G. & T. A. Wolfer (2000). Megachurch Involvement in Community Social Ministry: Extent and Effects in Three Congregations. In *Charitable Choice: The Challenge and Opportunity for Faith-Based Community Services*. D. A. Sherwood (Ed.). Botsford: North American Association of Christians in Social Work: 130-149.

Tobin, S. S., J. W. Ellor, & S.M. Anderson-Ray. (1986). *Enabling the Elderly*. Albany: State University of New York Press.

Veroff, J. & R. A. Kulka (1981). *Mental Health in America: Patterns of Help-Seeking from 1957-1976*. New York: Basic Books.

Faith-Related Agencies
and Their Implications for Aging Services

F. Ellen Netting, PhD

SUMMARY. The historical development of the faith-related organization is examined in light of the terminology used to describe these nonprofit groups, beginning with sectarian, moving to religious affiliate, and more recently using the term faith-related as a subcategory of being faith-based. Historical and contemporary research on faith-related organizations is reviewed, including a distinction between these studies and the increasing amount of research on religious congregations. Research findings are examined in the context of a complex political environment beginning with the Reagan/Bush Administrations, continuing into the Charitable Choice provisions introduced under the Clinton Administration, and moving to the Bush Administration's faith-based and community initiative. Implications of this initiative for the delivery of elder services are explored, particularly in light of the long-standing relationship the aging network has had with local faith groups. *[Article copies available for a fee from The Haworth Document Delivery Service: 1-800-HAWORTH. E-mail address: <docdelivery@haworthpress.com> Website: <http://www.HaworthPress.com> © 2004 by The Haworth Press, Inc. All rights reserved.]*

F. Ellen Netting is Professor, Virginia Commonwealth University School of Social Work, 1001 West Franklin Street, Richmond, VA 23284-2027 (E-mail: enetting@vcu.edu).

[Haworth co-indexing entry note]: "Faith-Related Agencies and Their Implications for Aging Services." Netting, F. Ellen. Co-published simultaneously in *Journal of Religious Gerontology* (The Haworth Pastoral Press, an imprint of The Haworth Press, Inc.) Vol. 16, No. 1/2, 2004, pp. 37-65; and: *Faith-Based Initiatives and Aging Services* (ed: F. Ellen Netting, and James W. Ellor) The Haworth Pastoral Press, an imprint of The Haworth Press, Inc., 2004, pp. 37-65. Single or multiple copies of this article are available for a fee from The Haworth Document Delivery Service [1-800-HAWORTH, 9:00 a.m. - 5:00 p.m. (EST). E-mail address: docdelivery@haworthpress.com].

http://www.haworthpress.com/web/JRG
© 2004 by The Haworth Press, Inc. All rights reserved.
Digital Object Identifier: 10.1300/J078v16n01_03

KEYWORDS. Sectarian, religious affiliate, faith-based, Charitable Choice, human services

Recently I was asked my view about the introduction of the faith-based and community initiative. The question was intended to be provocative, in that it was asked by someone not at all convinced that this was a good thing. I responded that certainly one could argue about the details of why this initiative was proposed and the contextual politics, but that I choose to see it as an incredible opportunity for public discourse. When I conducted my studies of religious affiliates during the 1980s (Netting, 1982a, 1982b, 1984a, 1984b, 1987, 1991), faith-based provision of services had not yet captivated the national agenda. Although the Reagan Administration was proposing that churches should take a more active role in caring for the poor in their communities, the complexity of this seemingly simple proposal had not yet been fully realized. Even under the Clinton Administration, the Charitable Choice provision in the welfare reform act was merely one piece of a controversial debate. However, with the introduction of the faith-based and community initiative, the topic riveted the nation's attention as a centerpiece of the Bush Administration's early days. It is heartening to be at this stage of my career, looking back on the concept of religious affiliation in light of the faith-based debate. No matter where one stands politically, no one interested in religion or human services can escape the dialogue. And after years of being fascinated by the complexity of the situation, it is worth the wait to see others engage the issues as well.

Central to that debate is the question of what is a faith-based organization. Some persons are using the term *faith-based* in its broadest sense–any organization that claims to have a commitment to a belief system no matter how loosely defined. Others are using the term in a more focused manner, referring to those organizations called religious congregations around which faith traditions organize their activities. Still others are seeing faith-based as a politically correct term to promote their own agendas. And there are definitely multiple agendas! Because people are using *faith-based* in so many ways and meanings are evolving, clear communication is a challenge.

In this article, I explore the historical development of terminology used to describe those formal services and programs provided in the name of a faith-based group, but which are typically incorporated as separate nonprofits from their parent religious bodies. This exploration assumes a journey in which various terms emerge and wane, and in which researchers attempt to capture the essence of these illusive concepts. Next I examine the complex political environment in which these terms are batted about in the controversial nature of public discourse. Most importantly, I will examine the implications for those organizations that serve older persons within a changing landscape of human service provision.

AN HISTORICAL PERSPECTIVE: FROM SECTARIAN TO FAITH-BASED

Emergence of the Sectarian Agency

As early as the 1700s, a parallel development of church-related and secular private charities occurred in the United States. These providers typically offered both material assistance as well as moral instruction to the poor (Bremmer, 1964). Although before the turn of the century there were few Catholic and Jewish groups in the U.S., some of the first residential institutions for orphans and elders were created by Roman Catholic orders. The first of these organizations was established by Ursuline Sisters in New Orleans in 1727. These establishments were "American transplants" of European efforts by Catholic orders in Europe (Reid & Stimpson, 1987).

Yet, Protestantism dominated early church-related providers, and because Protestants were so diverse and autonomous each denomination developed its own set of agencies (Reid & Stimpson, 1987). Given this domination, large numbers of Catholic immigrants who came to this country in the 1800s were fearful of being proselytized. Their fears were validated when religious human service agencies were often used as a means to convert the masses. These concerns led to the proliferation of sectarian agencies that were designed to target one's own faith group and to preserve the integrity of a particular religious community (Loewenberg, 1988).

The roles of organizations having affiliations with faith communities has been discussed for centuries, leading one writer in 1884 to observe that "the lack of a definition for the term 'sectarianism' is noteworthy. No one admits to it themselves. Many institutions having no trace of sectarianism in charter, constitution, or by-laws, are yet administered in the interests of a sect" (Warner, 1894, pp. 339-340). Warner's study revealed that sectarian and non-sectarian charities did not have clear distinctions, but that there were discernible differences between public and private charities. Over a century later, Hall reflects on Warren's work, saying that "Surprisingly little has changed since Warner wrote" (2001, p. 80).

For the purposes of this article, sectarian means related to a sect, and a sect in this case is a religious body. However, it is important to note that in earlier times sectarian was used to mean that an agency served only clients associated with its religious group. Technically, sectarian could be used to define any agency sponsored or affiliated with a specific group, religious or ethnic (Teicher, 1972, p. 79).

During the early days of welfare provision, sectarian agencies emerged in all areas of health and human services, whether they were health care institutions such as hospitals and nursing homes, or home and community-based services such as family counseling or home care agencies. Depending on the individual organization, the meaning of sectarianism varied greatly. For example, some agencies (primarily Protestant) were so loosely linked with a parent religious body that their members had difficulty fully explaining what their sectarian status meant. Other agencies had clearer guidelines for how to maintain their ties with the parent religious body. Historical scrutiny reveals great diversity among sectarian agencies.

The Proliferation of Private Charities

Many private charity organizations developed between 1870 and 1910. Private agencies had arisen sporadically since early Colonial times, directing their efforts toward specific religious or nationality groups. The earliest Protestant Church charity that had become permanent was the Boston Quarterly Lecture, established in 1720. It was Mary Richmond, a social work pioneer, who wrote that "The Church furnishes us with motive for all our work . . . and sends us forward . . . in a campaign that involves wider issues" (cited in Coughlin, 1965, p. 22). These words echoed as Protestants created umbrella agencies for human services, Catholic charities emerged in diocesan and national centers, and Jewish community centers and family service agencies proliferated during the early 1900s (Chambers, 1985). There were so many private agencies working at cross purposes that an organizational mechanism was necessary (Miles, 1949, p. 142). Thus was born The Charity Organization Society (COS).

The COS movement was initiated by a minister, Stephen Humphreys Gurteen (Reid & Stimpson, 1987). According to Leiby (1984) the COS was somewhat of an "embarrassment" (p. 536) because it was a social movement initiated by people who believed that government had no place in social welfare and who had definite opinions about the deserving and undeserving poor. Nevertheless, Leiby indicates that one need not discard the COS workers and their well-meaning leaders. He explains that those involved in the COS "based their vision on religious dogma institutionalized in the practice of charity in their time. In bypassing the dogma, we should not overlook the vision" (1984, p. 536). Charity Organization Societies were designed to plan and organize private services. Gradually, however, as specialized voluntary service increased, the societies limited their functions, changed their names, and became family welfare associations (Cayton & Nishi, 1955, p. 25).

During the same period, another form of organization occurred at the neighborhood level. In his classic on the Social Gospel, Charles H. Hopkins states, "The most concrete organized product of the movement was the institutional church and the religious social settlement" (1940, p. 319). In 1886 Stanton Coit established the first American settlement house in New York City. The settlement movement had its religious influences as well. Many of the persons who embraced the settlement movement were prominent religious leaders (Westby, 1985). As the settlement movement spread rapidly, there emerged an ongoing debate regarding whether or not a settlement should be religiously affiliated. In 1907 an entire issue of the *Annals of the American Academy of Political and Social Science* was dedicated to the social work of the Church. Proponents of the Social Gospel compelled individual laypeople to develop social service networks and even pushed government to take responsibility for those unaccommodated by voluntary agencies (Berger & Neuhaus, 1977, p. 235). Possibly it was leaders like Jane Addams who tempered this religious zeal among settlement house workers.

With the systematization of community-wide fundraising for welfare, sectarian agencies found themselves in competition with non-sectarian programs. Between 1900 and World War I many agencies experimented with federated financing. Sectarian agencies were noteworthy in this respect. In 1909 the Brooklyn Federation of Jewish Charities was created and in 1917 the much larger New York Federation of Jewish Philanthropic Societies was established. The National Conference on Catholic Charities began in 1910 and developed as a link for 545 diocesan agencies and 200 member agencies in the United States. However, the control in agency relationships rested primarily with local diocesan leadership rather than under national auspices (Reid & Stimpson, 1987). In 1931 the Federation of Protestant Agencies Caring for Protestants formed a fundraising department (Cayton & Nishi, 1955,

p. 49). In 1941 War Chests in over 400 communities organized, later to become Community Chests and Councils of America, Inc. "Thus the church's distinctive role and contribution to social welfare became a serious concern to both religious and professional interests" (Cayton & Nishi, 1955, p. 49). In fact, some Protestant agencies, with their diversified ideas and activities, dropped their church connections. Catholic and Jewish services, on the other hand, proved more organized and consistent in maintaining their religious identification.

Changes in Public-Private Relationships

In the early part of the 20th century two major theoretical views of the relationships between public and private agencies emerged. Since sectarian agencies comprised a large portion of the private social service sector, these theoretical debates were relevant to their concerns. In 1908 Benjamin K. Gray presented the "parallel bars concept of voluntary welfare," explaining the situation as one where voluntary agencies are "viewed as a pioneering yardstick and advocate, by which to measure similar government services" (Kahn, 1976, p. 49).

In 1914 Sidney Webb described a relationship whereby the voluntary agency should be used by government as an "extension ladder placed firmly on the foundation of an enforced minimum standard of life, and carrying onward the work of the public authorities to far finer shades of physical, moral and spiritual perfection. . . . In the public authority, the voluntary agencies discover a partner who is willing to remain in the background, but who has the necessary resources" (p. 704). With the emphasis upon voluntary welfare, rather than public responsibility for dependent people, expedience dictated directing public funds through private agencies. The subsidy system, in which public funds were channeled through private charities, became so entrenched that a clearcut policy in relation to public and private agencies did not emerge until 1933 (Miles, 1949, pp. 142-150).

The depression years brought the public partner out of hiding. With the 1933 establishment of the Federal Emergency Relief Act, Harry Hopkins declared that government funds would be spent only by public agencies (Miles, 1949, p. 150). In the 1930s social workers moved from voluntary to public agencies. The relationship now became one of the public *versus* the private sector (Mayo, 1960, p. 1). Within the voluntary sector there were strains as well. Clergy, the prime movers of sectarian social work at its inception, were being replaced by social work careerists, whose practice was influenced more by a professional rather than a religious orientation (Reid, 1977).

Between 1950 and 1967 public programs moved from spending less than voluntary agencies to spending twice as much (Burd & Richmond, 1979, p. 219). But by the 1950s the federal policy of total separation began to erode. A shift from public *versus* private to public *and* private occurred. After 1950 medical services could be purchased by the private sector. After World War II voluntary agencies were increasingly used for federal research and demonstration projects, first in mental health, juvenile delinquency, housing, community development, and later through the Office of Economic Opportunity (OEO) and its War on Poverty programs. Voluntary child welfare programs experienced a boost in 1961 when purchase of foster care was approved. The 1962 Amendments to the Social Security Act mentioned "social services" for the first time and the importance attached to them was emphasized by an increased federal contribution to the State (Wickenden, 1976, p. 580).

Although the 1962 Amendments rejected direct purchase of service from the voluntary sector, funds could be transferred from state agencies to voluntary services. In 1967 the old restrictions were dropped and the Amendments to the Social Security Act established the authority to purchase social services directly from voluntary organizations (Wickenden, 1976). This policy shift continued under Title XX. As government support increased, regulations regarding the purpose, program, clientele, staff and board composition of voluntary agencies were introduced (Berger, 1976, p. 240). This intermingling of funds caused sectarian agencies and institutions, as part of the voluntary sector, to seriously question their relationships to parent religious bodies and to government since they had begun to receive monies from varied sources. Given the proliferation of secular institutions of welfare, both private and public, and given the increase in the public role that occurred during the middle part of the 20th century, it became more and more difficult for sectarian organizations to define who they were in relation to Church and State.

In 1971 Hill declared that U.S. developments in social welfare had followed one of two directions, either the secularization of organizations begun under religious auspices or inspired by religious motives, or the maintenance and development of sectarian organizations. For those sectarian organizations that maintained their ties with faith traditions or parent religious bodies, their roles were becoming even more difficult to define. Sectarian was often used to describe an agency that served only clients associated with the group to which the agency related, yet there were sectarian agencies that had never served just their own. Some organizations proudly used the term, whereas others viewed sectarianism as an indicator of discriminatory practice. The sectarian agency, being a subcategory of the voluntary agency, faced the same difficulties of blurred roles, mixed funding, ambiguous concepts, accountability questions, and issues of autonomy. Many agencies, originally begun by a religious group, lost those religious ties. For those who continued to acknowledge a tie to a faith community, yet were considered "public" in terms of whom they served, identity questions were rising.

Attempting to Define Sectarian Agencies

In the 20th century, the sectarian agency had taken a variety of forms. Reid wrote that "It is possible in a rough way to place any church-related agency along a sectarian-secular continuum, using such indexes as the degree of control by the parent religious body, the relative amount of financial support accruing from sectarian sources, the proportion of board members who are of the faith, the extreme to which the actions of the organization's decision-makers are guided by religious considerations, the amount of religious content in service programs, and the religious identification of its clientele" (1977, p. 1251).

The religious bodies to which sectarian agencies were related also varied considerably. Ernst Troeltsch (1931) distinguished between two categories of religious groups: the church and the sect. Defined as large, mature and socially acceptable, churches were viewed as divided into ecclesia (universal religions), denominations, or bureaucratic types. These types were: (1) the episcopal (local responsibility to the upper hierarchy), (2) the presbyterian (local responsibility to a local body), and (3) the congregational (self-governing). Sects, on the other hand, were considered to be small and unstructured (Nottingham, 1954, pp. 67-68).

In the last century, several themes emerged in the development of sectarian welfare services. As Protestant agencies developed services, their tendency toward individualism and autonomy meant that patterns were not easy to discern. These agencies had diverse connections to their parent religious bodies, often difficult to distinguish in terms of authority and form. Clergy acting independently of the church or laypersons inspired by religious convictions were as likely to develop an organized vehicle for service delivery as was an agency to be established by a formal organizational mandate at the denominational level. These amorphous and loose ties often led to secularization of Protestant agencies, but also allowed the autonomy necessary to engage in social action and social reform. The Social Gospel movement at the turn of the century was instrumental in supporting Protestant social welfare initiatives (Reid & Stimpson, 1987).

Catholic agencies were much more tightly structured than their Protestant counterparts. Tied to established service orders and to a hierarchical ecclesiastical structure, Catholic organizations were much more defined. Much focus was placed on the development of institutions such as homes for dependent children, orphanages, and schools. Fears that Catholics would be subject to Protestant evangelism perpetuated the closer affiliations established by these religious agencies to their parent religious body. Reid and Stimpson (1987) point out, for example, that the homeless children who were sent to the midwest by the Reverend Charles Brace and his colleagues were often Catholic children who were sent to Protestant homes. This tension between Protestant and Catholic agencies and their leadership was reinforced when Catholic welfare efforts were reimbursed with public dollars for the care of their children. "Such opposition stimulated Catholic leaders to play a more active role in the politics of welfare and fostered the development of Catholic welfare organizations at both local and national levels" (Reid & Stimpson, 1987, p. 547).

Similar to the Catholic expansion following waves of immigration, Jewish welfare agencies expanded rapidly as more Jews arrived from European countries. However, Jewish welfare efforts were distinctive from other sectarian groups. These agencies were *not religious affiliates* in that these organizations were created separately from the synagogues as expressions of Jewish cultural needs rather than as solely religiously motivated services. It is not that Jewish welfare services were completely secular, it is just important to recognize that common ethnic roots and responses to anti-Semitism from the dominant Protestant culture led to a blending of religious and community human service needs (Reid & Stimpson, 1987).

There is no distinctive point at which the term sectarianism can be said to have gone out of vogue, although it is remarkable today how dated the term sounds when spoken aloud. The concept of *sect* was always somewhat questionable, given the tendency to think of a sect as small and potentially non-mainstream. And no doubt the concept of sect became especially problematic in light of the numbers of sects highlighted in the media in a less than positive light over the last number of decades. Whatever the reasons, by the time I was conducting my research in the early 1980s, sectarian agencies were in transition, searching for terms other than sectarian to describe themselves.

STUDIES OF FAITH-RELATED AGENCIES

One of the first attempts to better understand sectarian human service organizations and their structures was made in 1955 by the National Council of Churches. They found that Jewish agencies tended to carry a heavier burden of the social welfare responsibility in urban areas in serving persons of their own and other faith traditions. Catholics tended to focus on taking care of their own, and Protestants were viewed as difficult to track because their efforts were so diverse. It was revealed that the Church had lost a number of agencies to secularization. Among those agencies still affiliated, there was tension when church control was strong but financial support was weak. The most striking finding was that "no matter what dimension [was] taken, there [did] not appear readily a pattern of what might be typical or what might be generally true of protestanism, except for the fact of range" in social welfare involvement (Cayton & Nichi, 1955, p. 8).

In 1961 an examination of service statistics reported by church related programs revealed that sectarian services were continuing to change. "We do not have sectarian agencies serving a predominately sectarian clientele with a sharply defined sectarian orientation and with substantial financing" (Morris, 1961, p. 48). One survey of planning groups in forty-six cities indicated that most sectarian agencies were United Fund members, showing leadership and innovativeness in their programs. There was evidence that the relationships between sectarian federations and central planning bodies was one-sided in favor of church-related agencies (Tropman, 1961).

An extensive study was conducted by Coughlin in the early 1960s. Surveying 407 sectarian agencies in twenty states revealed that 70 percent were involved in some form of government contracting. Despite ideological opposition of some national church leaders, 89 percent of local agency executives saw no conflict between principles of church-state separation and purchase of service contracting. Coughlin indicated that 53 percent of voluntary health and welfare agencies had no written policy regarding public financing and concluded that the churches needed to formulate policies regarding their relationships with government (1965, p. 63). And lest anyone thinks that the questions about how the receipt of public dollars impacts voluntary agencies (a large group of which are religiously based) is new, studies examining the impact of public dollars on these agencies were also being conducted in the 1970s (see for example Kramer, 1981). These concerns were evident to practitioners and scholars long before the issues became fodder for public discourse.

During the late 1970s the United Methodists experienced the Pacific Homes litigation, and this became the motivating force for me to pursue a study of the meaning of religious affiliation. Several retirement homes affiliated with the United Methodist Church had severe financial difficulties. Settled out of court for $21 million, this experience caused leaders in The Health and Welfare Ministries of the United Methodist Church to publish a guide on the relationship between their jurisdictional units and their religious affiliates (Gaffney & Sorensen, 1984). Each institution was encouraged to determine what relationship they could negotiate and the implications of having denominational endorsements was analyzed legally. "The statement regarding the church's debt liability depicts a growing trend to protect churches in an era in which charitable immunity (freedom from lawsuit) is a thing of the past" (Reid & Stimpson, 1987, p. 548).

In 1980-81 my dissertation work focused on three groups of service providers, their parent religious bodies, and their coordinating bodies in Chicago. The three groups included nine specialized Episcopal agencies, one large multi-service Lutheran agency with six locations, and seven agencies of The Salvation Army. Designed as three historical case studies, the intent of this study was to explore the meaning of religious affiliation for these organizations. Of particular interest was that one of these groups, The Salvation Army, was not an affiliate at all. The Salvation Army did not separately incorporate its local agencies. Even more important was that public dollars going to Army agencies was being given to The Salvation Army, a church in its own right, rather than being channeled through separate nonprofit corporations. The diversity among groups made for an intriguing comparison in that Episcopal and Army agencies had always served anyone in need, whereas the Lutheran agency, which was affiliated with the Missouri Synod, had very intentionally targeted only Missouri Synod Lutherans before becoming pan-Lutheran and eventually serving persons from all faiths. The historical trajectories of these agencies differed and the looseness or closeness of their ties with the parent religious body literally went from being one and the same (in the case of the Army) to such a loose arrangement that one Episcopal agency discovered in its history that they weren't serving anyone who was Episcopalian (Netting, 1984a). Questions of identity permeated the pages of documents and transcripts, with an overriding theme being the increasing percentages of agency budgets dependent on public funding (Netting, 1982a).

In this study, it was revealed that these religious agencies had multiple constituencies with whom they identified: the professional community, the community of service providers, the client community, and the religious community. Environmental trends including the move toward professionalization, shifts in public policy, funding changes, and broader societal attitudes influenced the communities with which agencies were most identified at different points in their historical development (Netting 1984b). Therefore, some organizations appeared much more identified with their parent religious bodies than others. This was reflected in the formal control exercised by parent bodies, manifested in legal authority and board composition. For example, whereas the Army had total control because the parent body *was* the agency's board, nonprofit affiliates in the other two denomination were less tied to their parent bodies. Board composition varied for the Lutherans and Episcopalians, with Lutheran agencies tending to have Lutheran board members and Episcopalians greatly varying among themselves. Minutes from one of the latter agencies actually revealed a dialogue that occurred when an agency's governing board mused over the identity of their agency in light of having just elected a Jewish president. Additional formal controls included fiscal accountability and property ownership (Netting, 1984a).

Informal influences were evident as well. Theology influenced decision-making in many of these agencies, sometimes quite subtly and other times less so. Denominational constituents who were leaders in the community and in the parent body were a source of belief system influence, as were clergy staff members, non-cleric staff who had commitments to the faith tradition and expectations about what that meant for agency operation, and the prevalence of religious programming (Netting, 1982b).

During the 1980s, I followed up my dissertation work with two studies designed to focus specifically on religious affiliates that provided housing and social services for older persons. Whereas in my dissertation research I looked at agencies that served a variety of population groups, these subsequent studies focused on the continuing care retirement community (CCRC) industry in which serious questions about the meaning of religious affiliation had arisen in the late 1970s and early 1980s, and which had actually motivated me to do my dissertation research.

In the mid-80s I conducted a study of nine CCRCs, exploring the meaning of religious affiliation for these providers of senior housing. Hoping to develop a typology of religious affiliates that could be tested in a larger study, it was surprising to find such variation in structural relationships. Among only nine organizations were seven distinctive models of religious affiliation: (1) affiliation with a religious order, (2) affiliation with a single congregation, (3) affiliation with multiple congregations of the same denomination, (4) affiliation with multiple congregations from two or more religious denominations, (5) begun by religious leaders but not officially sponsored by any particular church, synagogue, or denomination, (6) sponsored by a denomination, and (7) affiliated with a corporate intermediary (Netting, 1987).

In a follow-up study, I surveyed 284 religiously affiliated CCRCs in forty-two states. Structural arrangements between communities and their religious sponsors were difficult to categorize and no identifiable patterns emerged. One hundred and sixty-nine (60%) respondents indicated that their affiliation with a religious group had never implied financial liability by that group. Another thirty-eight (13%) reported that the parent religious body had been but was no longer responsible financially for debts. Forty-nine (17%) communities reported that their religious sponsors were financially liable. Ninety-seven (34%) respondents indicated that their denominations were building more retirement communities, and 182 (64%) said that their denominations were making elders a high priority. Advantages to religious affiliation were viewed as a consumer trust in the community and the opportunity to carry out the church's mission, gain access to residents, and market to seniors (Netting, 1991).

During the course of my dissertation and the subsequent research on CCRCs, a wave of related research was beginning. This research focused on direct provision of services by religious congregations. Specific to aging, the first national study attempting to categorize congregational programming had been conducted by the National Interfaith Coalition on Aging (1976). In 1986 Tobin, Ellor, and Anderson-Ray published their three-year study of six communities in which they divided programming for elders into four groups. In 1989 a national sample of Catholic parishes examined four categories of services (Lewis, 1989).

In the late 1980s and early 1990s national surveys were conducted with the intent of exploring the role of religious involvement in social services across population groups, with the unit of analysis being the religious congregation (see for example: McDonald, 1984; Salmon and Teitelbaum, 1984). Hodgkinson, Weitzman, and Kirsch (1988) produced a pivotal study for The Independent Sector, in which the activities of the nation's religious congregations were surveyed. Not surprisingly, congregations were involved in numerous programs designed to serve their local communities. Many congregations were also working with the established agencies of their denominations, leading the researchers to recommend that more studies examine these relationships. The followup research published by the Independent Sector was entitled *From Belief to Commitment: The Community Service Activities and Finances of Religious Congregations in the United States* (Hodgkinson, Weitzman, & Kirsch, 1993). A 1992-1995 Greensboro, North Carolina study of public and private agencies affirmed an increasing involvement in congregational resources since the Reagan Administration had begun, with social agencies using congregational volunteers and facilities (Wineburg, Ahmed, & Sills, 1997). Researchers began to turn their attention more and more to studies of congregations as faith-based providers (see for example: Ammerman, 2000; Chaves, 1999; Harris, 1999; Weber, 2000; Wineburg, 2001).

It was sometime in the last decade that the word of choice to describe those efforts that had once been called sectarian, and more recently had shifted to religiously affiliated, transitioned to become *faith-based*. Jeavons (1994) illustrated the difficulties inherent in measuring levels of religious commitment in those organizations that balanced belief systems with management principles. Smith and Sosin (2001) brought the concept up-to-date in their study of varieties of faith-related agencies. Unlike the numerous studies and writings focusing on congregations, they focus on the faith-related agency and ask the question: "Is faith important, and how is it important?" (p. 652). They define faith-related agencies "as social service organizations that have any of the following: a formal funding or administrative arrangement with a religious authority or authorities; a historical tie of this kind; a specific commitment to act within the dictates of a particular established faith; or a commitment to work together that stems from a common religion. These agencies have some link to religion at the institutional level, either directly or because some individuals act on the basis of their relation to a religious institution, not simply on the basis of their personal belief system" (Chaves 1994, as cited in Smith & Sosin, 2001, p. 652). Smith and Sosin's findings indicate that assumptions about faith-related organizations need closer examination. For example, the idea that small faith-based agencies are not as subject to secular culture and its influences is not substantiated. Neither is the assumption that large agencies are not driven by faith-based motivations. They contend that large faith-related agencies can deliver more services and "in some ways, most fully carry out faith missions that express the religious mission of the provision of help" (p. 665). Their study underscores the complexity involved in truly understanding the meaning of being faith-based.

Chambre's research continues the tradition of looking at the meaning of faith in organizations that emerge from religious belief systems. She carefully examines the historical development of four AIDS organizations in New York City, chronicling how their distinctive journeys change the nature of faith. She explains that "the eclectic spiritual stance of these organizations reflect broader trends in American religious life, such as interest in new age and non-Western approaches to understanding life, death, the process of dying; a tendency to shift denominational affiliations; and a willingness to borrow from various religious traditions" (2001, p. 451). The complexity of what it means to be faith-based is skillfully documented in this study as Chambre invites others to join the research effort "to explore the subtle and complex implications" (p. 452) of understanding those organizations called faith-based.

IDENTIFYING AND CATEGORIZING FAITH-BASED ORGANIZATIONS

The religious affiliate, now called faith-related, is one form of voluntary agency among diverse nonprofit and public organizations that make up the social welfare landscape. Prior to the 1980s the meaning of religious affiliation and sponsorship was not as pervasive in the voluntary sector literature. However, devolutionary trends beginning with the Reagan/Bush Administrations and accelerating in recent years, an increasing interest in nonprofit issues, national surveys of religious congregations, and increasing numbers of research studies position the faith-related organization to be the subject of renewed attention.

Even with renewed interest in voluntary agencies, it has been difficult to ascertain how many health and human service organizations are related to religious groups. Since most of these agencies are formally incorporated and therefore recognized in the eyes of state corporation commissions, it would seem that a simple state-by-state list could be generated. However, some agencies that have religious sounding names are not affiliated with any religious body, whereas other agencies that have secular sounding names may consider themselves to be faith-based. Also, as studies have pointed out, some agencies secularize and others return to their religious roots. The non-linear, sometimes unpredictable development of a faith-based organization, as with any organization, is ripe with change (Ellor, Netting, & Thibault, 1999).

The 1955 study by the National Council of Churches identified 2,783 health and welfare agencies (Cayton & Nishi, 1955). Obviously, these statistics are an historical snapshot since many religious agencies have secularized and others have been established over the last decades.

It would seem that one way to locate the number of religious affiliates would be to ask each religious group how many agencies they sponsor or endorse. In 1985 I contacted the national headquarters of religious groups in the United States and found approximately 14,000 organizations were reported to have a connection to the parent religious body. This simple logic fails when one realizes how diverse the structural relationships are, particularly among Protestant agencies. A church affiliate may be related to an order of nuns but have no formal relationship with the Catholic Church. Affiliates may be related to religious orders, jurisdictional units such as Conferences of the United Methodist Church, to independent groupings of churches representing one or more denominations, or to a group of laypeople and/or clergy who began the operation. There is no central database that categorizes agencies by their religious affiliations. Suffice it to say that 14,000 affiliates that relate to national bodies was a very conservative estimate (Netting, 1986).

In 1988 Loewenberg classified sectarian agencies into three groupings: (1) church sponsored agencies, (2) autonomous institutions, and (3) agencies sponsored by an ethnic community. Church sponsored agencies were related to local congregations, regional religious bodies or entire denominations. Examples are The Salvation Army and Catholic Charities. The second type, autonomous institutions, were viewed as legally independent (separate corporations) but had staff who remained closely tied to religious groups. Loewenberg described Lutheran agencies as representing this arrangement. The third type, agencies sponsored by ethnic groups, were viewed as "popularly identified with a religious group [or coexist] with a religious group. Thus most Jewish social agencies are not sponsored by or related to a synagogue, but are sponsored by the secular Jewish community" (Loewenberg, 1988, pp. 139-140). Ethnic agencies have been examined in detail by Jenkins (1980) as well. Other examples would be the Korean ethnic church and the services it sponsors and provides for Asian American immigrants (Hurh & Kim, 1990).

Cnaan and his colleagues (1999) expand the categorization of what are called *religious-based* social services according to their size and geographical scope. The six categories are: (1) local congregations, (2) interfaith agencies and ecumenical coalitions, (3) citywide or regionwide sectarian agencies, (4) national projects and organizations under religious auspices, (5) paradominational projects and organizations, and (6) religiously affiliated international organizations (p. 27).

The faith-related social service organization would primarily fall within the third of these categories: the citywide or regionwide sectarian agency. Cnaan goes on to identify a multitude of possible typologies based on different criteria, including the degree of close relationship with the parent religious body (from total dependence to full autonomy); or control over funding (from congregational control to a separate board of trustees); or according to the target population served (serving one's own or expanding to anyone in need). It is the complexity represented in the typologies suggested by Cnaan and his categories that reveal just how difficult it is to define the faith-related organization.

Even the federal agencies that grant funds to voluntary agencies are not certain how many of their grantees are faith-based. The Department of Health and Human Services (DHHS) reports that it can only underestimate the numbers of dollars going to faith-based organizations because "grantees do not report their affiliation in a manner that allows HHS to identify whether or not they are faith-based" (DHHS, 2001, p. 1). When states distribute funds through block or formula grants, they are not always required to report the faith-based nature of grantees. Because there is no government-wide definition of what a faith-based organization is, applicants are often categorized as nonprofit or community-based, leaving federal agencies without knowing if these local providers are faith-related.

Perhaps, it is not the numbers of organizations that are categorized as faith-related that is important, but understanding the context within which these organizations currently do their work. This calls for examining recent political debates about the roles of these organizations, followed by implications for aging service in American society.

CHARITABLE CHOICE AND THE FAITH-BASED AND COMMUNITY INITIATIVES

If the Reagan/Bush Administrations initiated a devolutionary trend, it was the Clinton Administration and the signing of the welfare reform act that sped up the process. At the time, the *Charitable Choice* provision, section 104 of PL 104-193 entitled the Personal Responsibility and Work Opportunity Reconciliation Act (PRWORA) of 1996, was one small part of a massive piece of legislation. In 1997 an amendment to PRWORA extended coverage of Charitable Choice to Welfare to Work programs administered by the Department of Labor, followed by a slightly different version passed into law in 1998 with the reauthorization of the Community Services Block Grant (CSBG). In 2000 charitable choice provisions were added to Federal substance abuse prevention and treatment programs under the DHHS Substance Abuse and Mental Health Services Administration (DHHS, 2001, p. 1). These provisions set the stage for the faith-based and community initiative.

Somewhat hidden in the vastness of welfare reform, Charitable Choice was the brainchild of then U.S. Senator John Ashcroft. One writer compares Charitable Choice to "a camel easing its nose under a tent" (Walsh, 2001, p. 1) because hardly anyone noticed at the time. This provision opened the door for states to contract with religious organizations on the same basis as any nongovernmental organization "without impairing the religious character of such organizations, and without diminishing the religious freedom of beneficiaries of assistance funded under such program" (Sherwood, 2000, p. 108). Charitable Choice was focused for the most part on the Temporary Assistance for Needy Families (TANF) programs that replaced Aid to Families with Dependent Children (AFDC), but it also applies to food stamps, Medicaid, and Supplemental Security Income (SSI). It was the intent of the Clinton Administration to encourage greater involvement of religious organizations in the provision of social welfare (Cnaan, 1999, pp. 281-282).

President George W. Bush issued Executive Order 13198 on January 29, 2001. This order created Centers for Faith-Based and Community Initiatives in five cabinet departments: Health and Human Services (HHS), Housing and Urban Renewal (HUD), Education (ED), Labor (DOL), and Justice (DOJ). Each Center was charged with conducting an audit of their departments to identify any barriers to participation by faith-based and other community organizations in delivery of social services (The White House, 2001, p. 1). Reaction was swift (see for example Daly & Dinnerman, 2001). Media coverage, think tank sponsored conferences, private foundation commitments to support new efforts by religious groups, research interest, and dinner table conversations focused around the intentions of this Executive Order. Yet, this was just the solidification of an ongoing effort already underway to expand the role of faith-based organizations in human service provision (Chambre, 2001, p. 436).

Arguments for and against the concept dominated public discourse in the early days of February 2001 and escalated when legislation was introduced into the House of Representatives. H.R. 7, The Charitable

Choice Act of 2001, became a lightening rod for raising the questions about the meaning of faith, the relationship between church and state in this country, and concerns about political intent. A broad coalition of religious, educational and civil rights groups opposed the bill in its original form. And as it moved to the Senate, there were great concerns about aspects of what was being proposed, including for example the possibility of exempting religious groups from discriminatory hiring even if they received public dollars, and the use of voucher systems that would not fund operational costs.

What these activities did mean is that the concept of faith-based had not only reached the public agenda, but it was high on its priority list. If the 1996 Charitable Choice provision was indeed a camel slipping its head under a tent (Walsh, 2001, p. 1), then 2001 was when the camel rose up and the tent came tumbling down. Exposed were a plethora of issues that had been debated in the literature and talked about in the corridors of faith-based organizations for decades. The public discourse had finally begun.

WHAT DOES THIS MEAN FOR AGING SERVICES?

Charitable Choice, first introduced in 1996 through the welfare reform act, was not designed to have a direct impact on older persons. Indirectly, it may have been felt by elders who were the parents and grandparents of TANF families, but the targeted population group was younger–parents who needed to find employment, and their children. Similarly, the rhetoric surrounding the faith-based and community initiative has been more focused on addressing social problems that pertain to younger age groups. Yet there are a number of very costly government programs that target elder needs.

Current Government Programs

The DHHS has a budget of $429 billion and is the largest grant-making agency in federal government, awarding 60,000 grants each year. Of those grants, 87% are mandatory in that DHHS is statutorily required to provide an award if an acceptable State Plan or application is submitted that meets required eligibility and compliance standards. Of DHHS mandatory grants, Medicare makes up 58% or $218.8 billion, and Medicaid makes up 33% or $124.8 billion (DHHS, 2001, p. 1). This means that Medicare and Medicaid represent 80% of the total DHHS budget and 91% of all mandatory grants. Medicare provides joint health insurance for 39 million elders and disabled Americans, whereas Medicaid is a joint federal-state program that provides health coverage for over 34 million low-income persons, including nursing home coverage for low-income elders. Both programs are within the Centers for Medicare and Medicaid Services (CMS), formerly the Health Care Financing Administration (HCFA) (DHHS, 2001, p. 6).

Health care systems and long-term care facilities that provide care to elders are recipients of third-party payments from Medicare and Medicaid. Many of these organizations were begun by religious groups and have maintained their affiliations. It is important to recognize that these public-private relationships have been an ongoing part of the service delivery system. Under state Medicaid waiver programs in which home and community-based care is provided, other organizations may be the recipients of public dollars for elder care. Again, some of these community-based providers may be faith-related nonprofits. The faith-based and community initiative is not intended to make congregations the providers of these highly professionalized health care services.

Besides Medicare and Medicaid, mandatory grants that specifically target elders include block grants that enable States to address specific citizen needs. For example, the Community Services Block Grant (CSBG) monies could be used by various states for some elder care services. Other mandatory grants include closed-ended grants, defined as awards that constitute "an upper limit on the amount of funds the Federal Government may pay for program activities" (DHHS, 2001, p. 2). Closed-ended grants are those channeled to state and local programs on aging under Title III of the Older Americans Act. It is important to note that only $1.1 billion constitutes the Administration on Aging (AoA) budget, the smallest budget of all Divisions within DHHS. The AoA budget is distributed through the aging network, and local Area Agencies on Aging typically grant monies to local providers for home and community-based services.

When one thinks about age-related home and community-based human services, the AoA is the likely place one looks. Anyone who has worked in the aging network recognizes how limited federal dollars have always been for programs mandated through the Older Americans Act. Area Agencies on Aging and their provider agencies have learned to live on limited public dollars, often pooling federal, state and local resources; mobilizing volunteers; and collaborating with other agencies to make ends meet. Some of these providers have long been faith-related organizations. Interestingly enough, this patchwork of aging services has always been mindful of faith-based efforts in their communities, working with local clergy who sit on their advisory and governing boards, asking local churches to serve as senior nutrition sites, recruiting volunteers from religious congregations, and a host of other activities. Because they have had to be skilled in community organizing, it comes as little surprise to those who have worked in the aging network that the faith-based and community initiative only reinforces what the aging network has done for years.

The White House Report

A report synthesizing the audits of the five cabinet departments mandated by Executive Order 13198 was published in August 2001.[1] In this report, three references were made to programs that directly target older persons: The Department of Labor's Senior Employment Program; HUD's Section 303 and 811 housing program; and The DHHS National Family Caregiver Support Program. Each is briefly reviewed below.

Example #1

Under a subheading titled *Routinized Granting Without Performance Monitoring*, The Department of Labor reported that "the same 11 large organizations have ranked among the top-10 grant recipients over the past five years" in the Senior Community Services Employment Program (The White House, 2001, p. 8). The senior employment program is among several cited as examples in which "apparent Federal Grant monopolists" often receive large grants "even though there is little empirical evidence substantiating the success of their services" (p. 8).

One implication here is that other potential providers need to be given the opportunity to compete with those organizations that have benefitted from multi-year, continuation grants. A second implication is that these established grantees have not conducted rigorous program evaluations even though outcome-based performance measurement is an accountability expectation. Certainly competition is a motivator for organizations to become more effective in their program delivery, but it is questionable that a new faith-based organization will have the capability to rigorously evaluate programs that seasoned agencies have had difficulty evaluating. Another question left unanswered is if any of those 11 large organizations are already faith-related providers. Conceivably, the rush to engage local faith-based organizations in service delivery could place them in competition for limited funding with established faith-related agencies in their own communities.

From the government side of the equation, it is clear that the audit of federal departments reveals a nagging concern that there are organizations that have become adept at writing and obtaining federal grants. Their monopolist efforts are being carefully viewed "with an eye to ensuring that expenditures yield the planned-for results in the lives of people who need help" (The White House, 2001, p. 2). There is concern that current grantees, many of whom are historically established faith-related nonprofits, are not producing the outcomes desired in a performance-based programming environment. Complicating the situation is that no federal definition of faith-based and community-based organizations exists, yet the numbers of charitable choice provisions are opening the doors for these undefined groups to compete for dollars. It does not appear that large numbers of new dollars will be forthcoming.

Example # 2

Under a subheading entitled *Faith-Based Organizations Excluded from Funding*, it is stated that "HUD's Section 202 and 811 programs that fund supportive residences for the elderly and for persons with disabilities, respectively, do not permit 'religious' organizations or ones that have religious purposes to be project owners, although they may be *sponsors* who initiate a project. This ownership restriction is stated explicitly in the program handbooks and is portrayed as a constitutional requirement, but it has neither a constitutional nor a statutory basis. (Ironically, over the more than 35-year history of the Section 202 program, more than two-thirds of the sponsors of the housing for the elderly have been religious organizations)" (p. 12). The report goes on to say that religious organizations are faced with an unwelcoming environment in which faith groups are not allowed to be overtly religious.

Opening the door for religious groups to own supportive residences for elders and person with disabilities is fraught with complexity. Let's briefly return to the late 1970s and early 1980s when the issue of who owned elder housing riveted the attention of anxious religious denominations. At that time retirement communities affiliated with mainline groups were experiencing financial difficulties. These were homes established by the religious community with every good intention of offering services to older persons. Religious leaders learned that providing services requires business acumen as well as spiritual compassion. Lawyers assisted them in figuring out ways to legally structure these corporations separate from their religious denominations. Clergy leaders either gained management expertise in addition to their theological education or persons with business backgrounds were hired as administrators. It was a time in which the importance of *both* genuine religious motivation and administrative skill were recognized. Faith alone, no matter how strong, could not adequately manage these nonprofit organizations.

For the older residents of these communities hard lessons were learned. Their assumptions about what it meant to move into a faith-related community were tested. No one knows if these same residents would have moved into these facilities had they been secular rather than religiously sponsored, and it is too late to ask them that question. However, it became clear that marketing to older persons in the name of a faith tradition was far more complex than originally conceived. Whatever the faith-relationship of these retirement communities meant, one can be sure it was redefined for residents who lived through the bankruptcies.

Today, parent religious bodies vary greatly in their legal responsibilities toward their human service affiliates. Some religious groups entered the 1990s with their eyes open, ready to back their agencies even at the expense of a lawsuit. Other religious groups have assessed the situation and decided to back away from their fiscal responsibilities, indicating that affiliates may be endorsed but that this does not carry the full weight of financial liability with it. In the wake of the Pacific Homes case, religious groups began to reexamine their responsibilities. Some agencies were advised to remove the names of their parent body from legal documents, even from stationary where logos implied the backing of a faith community. It is within this nest of issues that housing ownership versus sponsorship must be considered.

Example # 3

The third reference specific to elder programming is listed under a subheading called *Barrier 13: An Inappropriate Requirement to Apply in Collaboration with Likely Competitors*. A number of federal programs require local providers to demonstrate collaboration with other community agencies, even though these same agencies may be in competition for the same funding. Each of the five departments identified at least one program that had an anti-competitive application requirement, and the DHHS listed The National Family Caregiver Support Program. This initiative required any applicant for funding to obtain the support of the local Area Agency on Aging, but subsequently the Administration on Aging removed this condition.

In this third reference, the identified barrier was removed by AoA. However, it raises an interesting point. If the Area Agency on Aging is a competitor with local providers for funding for The National Family Caregiver Support Program then what happens when that same local provider responds to a request for proposals (RFP) from the AAA. Perhaps a barrier is limited resources that cannot adequately cover the needs of elders and their caregivers. This example reflects a major concern about the faith-based initiative–that as long as local providers compete for limited public dollars, they will not have the time to join forces in advocating for a greater pool of resources for population groups in need. The more potential providers who can be mobilized to write grants, the less time anyone will have to engage in social reform.

A continuing programmatic audit to identify and reduce barriers to faith-based groups continues within the departments of government. Perhaps one of the reasons elders are not the primary stakeholders in this process is that the bulk of federal dollars targeting their needs are going to health insurance programs (Medicare and Medicaid). Local congregations and small community-based groups are not equipped, nor do they necessarily want to be, to provide the kinds of services reimbursed by these large programs. Yet, when it comes to aging network services, local faith-based groups are critical players.

CONCLUSION

Faith-related retirement homes, assisted living facilities, senior citizens' groups, hospitals and nursing homes begun by religious orders or sponsored by religious denominations dot the landscape of local communities. There is nothing new about being faith-based (Marty, 1980). What is new is that the landscape is becoming more and more complex given the sheer numbers of elders and their plurality; the diversification of programs and services; the spirituality movement that transcends religious difference; and the diverse philosophical, political and economic motivations that drive an informed set of stakeholders. What else is new is the political focus on the faith group itself as provider, combined with an increasing skepticism that traditional faith-related organizations are part of a monopolistic cadre of grantees who have captured public dollars.

Wittberg (2000) illustrates just how complicated the situation is when she reframes the question: "although much has been written about [religious] institutions losing their religious identify, few studies explore the implications of religions losing their institutional identity" (p. 357). Noting that parent religious bodies have sponsored faith-related institutions and services as a way of living their faith, she observes that these sponsored agencies have been the public face that gives visibility to the denomination's mission. Rather than just focusing on what it means to be faith-related, a more important question may be: what does it mean for the identity of established faith communities when their established vehicles of service delivery are being seen as less than accountable? What happens when congregations are encouraged to compete for limited funds with long-established faith-related providers? Most importantly, what does all of this political maneuvering mean for elders who need services?

In previous years, sectarian agencies were separate, nonprofit corporations. Even if only one local congregation was a sponsor, sponsorship implied an affiliation. They were religious affiliates. In today's parlance, they are faith-related. This is different from being one and the same corporation, a combined ministry and agency. The current movement toward funding faith-based organizations opens a door that was only previously cracked. Groups like The Salvation Army and Volunteers of America are religious groups who have directly received funding from government for years, but it was not general public knowledge that these were religious groups receiving public dollars. Even more importantly, their religious missions were tied to a social service orientation that was almost inseparable. Therefore, precedents have been set for directly funding religious groups to provide services. What is different is that local congregations of all faith traditions represent incredibly diverse capabilities when it comes to applying for and managing public dollars. Many of these congregations are not incorporated as nonprofit organizations. So the door is now opening wider for faith-based groups who have never considered public dollars. This is the *level playing field* to which President Bush has referred over and over again. It is important that these new players are savvy in knowing that faith must be complemented by managerial capability, a lesson learned from the rich historical legacy of the sectarian/religious affiliate.

The aging network has always survived on a shoestring and its ability to collaborate with grassroots organizations, faith-based and secular, is ongoing. The faith-related agencies that have survived for decades will continue to change. Some will secularize, others will return to the protective wing of their denominational sponsor, others will maintain a sense of continuity, and still others will disappear altogether. For the practitioner who works with elders it will be important to recognize the incredible complexity that surrounds the constellation of service providers and to be prepared to skillfully navigate an increasingly diverse delivery system.

NOTE

1. This report makes numerous points and deals with multiple programs and barriers. I have intentionally pulled the few references to programs that target elders and have not attempted to analyze the entire report and the numerous barriers identified. The interested reader is encouraged to read the full report in order to fully comprehend the issues discussed.

REFERENCES

Ammerman, N.T. (2000, November). *Congregations and their partners in social service delivery: Method and findings from the organizing religious work project.* Paper presented at the meeting of the Association for Research on Nonprofit Organizations and Voluntary Action, New Orleans.

Berger, G. (1976). American Jewish communal service 1776-1976: From traditional self-help to increasing dependence on government support. *Jewish Social Studies, 38,* 225-246.

Berger, P.L., & Neuhaus, R.J. (1977). *To empower people: The role of mediating in public policy.* Washington, D.C.: American Enterprise Institute for Public Policy Research.

Bremmer, R. H. (1964). *From the depths: The discovery of poverty in the United States.* New York: New York University Press.

Burd, R.P., & Richmond, J.B. (1979). Public and private sector: A developing partnership in human services. *American Journal of Orthopsychology, 29,* 218-229.

Cayton, H. & Nishi, S.M. (1955). *Churches and social welfare: The changing scene.* New York: National Council of Churches of Christ in the U.S.A.

Chambers, C.A. (1985). The historical role of the voluntary sector in human service delivery in urban America. In G.A. Tobin (Ed.). *Social planning and human service delivery in the voluntary sector* (pp. 3-28). Westport, CT: Greenwood Press.

Chambre, S.M. (2001). The changing nature of "faith" in faith-based organizations: Secularization and ecumenicism in four AIDS organizations in New York City. *Social Service Review, 75*(3), 435-455.

Chaves, M. (1994). Secularization as declining religious authority. *Social Forces, 72*(3), 749-774.

Chaves, M. (1998). The religious ethic and the spirit of nonprofit enterpreneurship. In W.W. Powell & E.S. Clements (Eds.). *Private Action and the Public Good* (pp. 47-68). New Haven, CT: Yale University Press.

Coughlin, B.J. (1965). *Church and state in social welfare.* New York: Columbia University Press.

Cnaan, R.A., with R.J. Wineburg and S.C. Boddie. (2000). *The newer deal: Social work and religion in partnership.* New York: Columbia University Press.

Daly, A., & Dinerman, M. (2001). Faith in the faith-based initiative? *Affilia, 16*(4), 405-410.

Department of Health and Human Services (DHHS). (July 27, 2001). *Report to the White House for faith-based and community initiatives.* Washington, D.C.: Center for Faith-based & Community Initiatives.

Ellor, J.W., Netting, F.E., & Thibault, J.M. (1999). *Religious and spiritual aspects of human service practice.* Columbia, SC: University of South Carolina Press.

Gaffney, E.M., Jr., & Sorensen, P.C. (1984). *Ascending liability in religious and other nonprofit organizations.* Mercer Studies in Law and Religion 2. Georgia: Center for Constitutional Studies and Mercer University Press.

Hall, P.D. (2001). Historical perspectives on religion, government and social welfare in America. In A. Walsh (Ed.). *Can charitable choice work? Covering religion's impact on urban affairs and social services* (pp. 78-120). The Pew Program on Religion and the News Media, The Leonard E. Greenberg Center for the Study of Religion in Public Life. Hartford, CT: Trinity College.

Harris, M. (1999). *Organizing God's work: Challenges for churches and synagogues.* New York: St. Martin's Press.

Hill, W.G. (1971). Voluntary and governmental finance transactions. *Social Casework, 52,* 356-361.

Hodgkinson, V.A., Weitzman, M.S., & Kirsh, A.D. (1988). *From belief to commitment: The community service activities and finances of religious congregations in the United States: Finds from the national survey.* Washington, D.C.: The Independent Sector

Hodgkinson, V.A., Weitzman, M.S., & Kirsh, A.D. (1993). *From belief to commitment: The community service activities and finances of religious congregations in the United States.* Washington, D.C.: The Independent Sector.

Hopkins, C.H. (1940). *The rise of the social gospel in American Protestanism 1865-1915.* New Haven, CT: Yale University Press.

Hurh, W.M. & Kim, K. C. (1990). Religious participation of Korean immigrants in the United States. *Journal for the Scientific Study of Religion, 29*(2), 19-34.

Jeavons, T.S. (1994). *When the bottom line is faithfulness: Management of Christian service organizations.* Bloomington, IN: Indiana University Press.

Jenkins, S. (1980). The ethnic agency defined. *Social Service Review, 54*(2), 249-261.

Kahn, A.J. (1976). A framework for public-voluntary collaboration in social services. *Social Welfare Forum.* New York: Columbia University Press.

Kramer, R.M. (1981). *Voluntary agencies in the welfare state.* Berkeley, CA: University of California Press.

Leiby, J. (1984, December). Charity organization reconsidered. *Social Service Review, 58*(4), 523-538.

Lewis, M.A. (1989). *Religious congregations and the informal supports of the frail elderly.* New York: The Third Age Center, Fordham University.

Loewenberg, F.M. (1988). *Religion and social work practice in contemporary American society.* New York: Columbia University Press.

MacDonald, C.B. & Luckett, J.B. (1983). Religious affiliation and psychiatric diagnosis. *Journal for the Scientific Study of Religion, 22,* 15-37.

Marty, M.E. (1980). Social service: Godly and godless. *Social Service Review, 54*(4), 463-481.

Mayo, L.W. (1960). Relationships between public and voluntary health and welfare agencies. *Child Welfare, 39,* 1-5.

McDonald, J.A. (1984). Survey finds religious groups strongly favor more collaboration. *Foundation News, 9,* 20-24.

Miles, A.P. (1949). *An introduction to public welfare.* Boston: D.C. Heath and Company.

Morris, R. (1961). Current directions in sectarian welfare in America. *Journal of Jewish Communal Service, 38,* 5-10.

Netting, F.E. (1984a). Church-related agencies and social welfare. *Social Service Review, 58*(3), 404-420.

Netting, F.E. (1987). Religiously affiliated continuum of care retirement communities. *Journal of Religion and Aging, 4*(1), 51-65.

Netting, F.E. (1982a). Secular and religious funding of church-related agencies. *Social Service Review, 56,* 586-604.

Netting, F.E. (1982b). Social work and religious values in church-related social agencies. *Social Work and Christianity, 9*(1-2), 4-20.

Netting, F.E. (1984b). The changing environment: Its effect on church-related agencies. *Social Work and Christianity, 2*(1), 16-30.

Netting, F.E. (1991). The meaning of church affiliation for continuum of care retirement communities. *The Journal of Religious Gerontology, 8*(2), 79-99.

Netting, F.E. (1986). The religious agency: Implications for social work administration. *Social Work and Christianity, 13*(2), 50-63.

Nottingham, E.K. (1954). *Religion and society.* New York: Random House.

Ortiz, L.P. (1995). Sectarian agencies. *Encyclopedia of social work,* 19th edition. Washington, D.C.: The National Association of Social Workers Press, pp. 2109-2116.

Reid, W.J. (1977). Sectarian agencies. *Encyclopedia of social work.* Washington, D.C.: The National Association of Social Workers.

Reid, W.J. & Stimpson, P. (1987). Sectarian agencies. *Encyclopedia of social work.* Washington, D.C.: The National Association of Social Workers.

Salamon, L.M. & Teitelbaum, F. (1984). Religious congregations as social service agencies: How extensive are they? *Foundation News, 5,* 2-4.

Sherwood, D.A. (Ed.). (2000). *Charitable choice: The challenge and opportunity for faith-based community services.* Botsford, CT: North American Association of Christians in Social Work.

Smith, E. P. (1995). Willingness and resistance to change: The case of the race discrimination amendment of 1942. *Social Service Review, 69*(1), 31-56.

Smith, S.R., & Sosin, M.R. (2001). The varieties of faith-related agencies. *Public Administration Review, 61*(6), 651-670.

Teicher, M.I. (1972). Re-examination of the rationale of sectarian social work. *Social Casework, 53*, 78-84.

The White House. (August 2001). *Unlevel playing field: Barriers to participation by faith-based and community organizations in federal social service programs.* Washington, D.C.: The White House.

Tobin, S., Ellor, J., & Anderson-Ray, S. (1986). *Enabling the elderly: Religious institutions within the community service system.* Albany, NY: State University of New York Press.

Troeltsch, E. (1931). *The social teachings of the Christian churches*, vol. 2. London, England: George Allen and Unwin, Ltd.

Tropman, E. J. (1961). Trends in sectarian social work and their effect on community planning. *Journal of Jewish Communal Service, 38*, 60-68.

Walsh, A. (Ed.). (2001). *Can charitable choice work? Covering religion's impact on urban affairs and social services.* The Pew Program on Religion and the News Media, The Leonard E. Greenberg Center for the Study of Religion in Public Life. Hartford, CT: Trinity College.

Warner, A. (1894). *American Charities.* New York: Thomas Y. Crowell and Company.

Webb, S. (March 7, 1914). The extension ladder theory of the relation between voluntary philanthropy and state or municipal action. *Survey, 31*, 703-707.

Weber, M.A. (2000, November). *America's religious congregations: Measuring their contribution to society.* Paper presented at the meeting of the Association for Research on Nonprofit Organizations and Voluntary Action, New Orleans, LA.

Westby, O. (1985). Religious groups and institutions. In G.A. Tobin (Ed.) *Social planning and human service delivery in the voluntary sector* (pp. 47-73). Westport, CT: Greenwood Press.

Wickenden, E. (1976). A perspective on social services: An essay review. *Social Service Review, 50*, 570-585.

Wittberg, P. (2000). Called to service: The changing institutional identities of American denominations. *Nonprofit and Voluntary Sector Quarterly, 29*(3), 357-376.

Wineburg, B. (2001). *A limited partnership: The politics of religion, welfare, and social service.* New York: Columbia University Press.

Wineburg, R.J., Ahmed, F., & Sills, M. (1997). Local human service organizations and the local religious community during an era of change. *Journal of Applied Social Sciences, 21*(2), 93-98.

Dialogue with Elizabeth Seale-Scott, Director, Center for Faith-Based and Community Initiatives, U.S. Department of Health and Human Services

James W. Ellor, PhD
F. Ellen Netting, PhD

The following dialogue occurred between Mrs. Elizabeth Seale-Scott, Dr. James W. Ellor, and Dr. F. Ellen Netting on August 29, 2001. Representatives from the Administration on Aging sat in during the dialogue since we were particularly interested in implications of the faith-based initiative for aging programs. The dialogue came after introductions had been made. The purpose of the dialogue was to promote understanding of the role and function of the new Center for Faith-Based and Community Initiatives.

SUMMARY. In an effort to fully understand the role of the office of Faith-Based Community Initiatives, in the U.S. Department of Health and Human Services, Drs. Netting and Ellor went to Washington, DC and interviewed the Director, Elizabeth Seale-Scott. This important dialogue is recorded here to further understand particularly the role of

[Haworth co-indexing entry note]: "Dialogue with Elizabeth Seale-Scott, Director, Center for Faith-Based and Community Initiatives, U.S. Department of Health and Human Services." Ellor, James W., and F. Ellen Netting. Co-published simultaneously in *Journal of Religious Gerontology* (The Haworth Pastoral Press, an imprint of The Haworth Press, Inc.) Vol. 16, No. 1/2, 2004, pp. 67-80; and: *Faith-Based Initiatives and Aging Services* (ed: F. Ellen Netting, and James W. Ellor) The Haworth Pastoral Press, an imprint of The Haworth Press, Inc., 2004, pp. 67-80. Single or multiple copies of this article are available for a fee from The Haworth Document Delivery Service [1-800-HAWORTH, 9:00 a.m. - 5:00 p.m. (EST). E-mail address: docdelivery@haworthpress.com].

this office as it impacts the Administration on Aging and Aging pro-grams. *[Article copies available for a fee from The Haworth Document Delivery Service: 1-800-HAWORTH. E-mail address: <docdelivery@haworthpress.com> Website: <http://www.HaworthPress.com> © 2004 by The Haworth Press, Inc. All rights re-served.]*

KEYWORDS. Congregations, level-playing field, Charitable Choice, public policy

Jim: The approach being taken by your Center appears to be an at-tempt to bring the faith-based concept to all of the various depart-ments and programs rather than targeting it at a single program area. Essentially, you want everyone to be conscious of this movement?

Elizabeth: Yes, because if you look down at the community level in my neighborhood, for example, in San Antonio, Texas, you have all of these tremendous providers, some are faith-based and some are community-based organizations. The ones I'm going to name are bigger–Big Brothers, Big Sisters, the Y, Lutheran Social Services, Catholic Charities–secular entities as well as the faith-based. They need to come together to complement one another in service to the community if they are going to make the greatest impact upon the community and not be duplicative. This whole initiative is very much geared toward that. Charitable Choice is geared toward faith-based groups. Historically, many faith-based organizations have not received government funding because government offi-cials thought they were too sectarian. Sometimes this may be war-ranted, but in many cases we find community healers and helpers providing valuable services through a strong sense of mission and yet they are not strong-arming people to do it as some may fear.

Ellen: I want to go back to a question that we should have started with and one that has been difficult to address. I'm not sure where the term faith-based came from and what it means. This is a very broad term. Is there someone who "coined" this term? Where did "faith-based" emerge as a concept and what made this the politically correct term?

Elizabeth: I'm wondering if Marvin Olasky's writings might be a starting place since he talks about the history of social services. I know he didn't coin the phrase, but I seem to recall that he made mention of it. The first time I heard it was in discussions about welfare reform and charitable choice because faith-based was broadly inclusive and could apply to Catholics, Muslims, Jews, Protestants–to everybody. The initiative is intended to be inclusive of all those entities (looks toward Jim) . . . You've had more experience in that area . . .

Jim: I know it's intended to be inclusive, but when you look at the theologies, the concept of faith is very important in Judaism, Islam, and Christianity, but is less important in some of the other world traditions. I think it is understood in the way you are using it . . . but it holds a whole different set of assumptions within different traditions.

Ellen: I'm sure the intent is to make things inclusive, and the whole country is using it. Faith-based seems to imply connected or based in something. I'm even wondering how it ties to the spirituality movement which can be connected to organized religion but can also be highly individualistic. And I've noted that we aren't using the term spiritual initiative here. I'm wondering, then, if the implication is that there should be a tie to some group or religion in terms of accountability. It's not just "faith" . . . it's "faith-based."

Elizabeth: Please take this in the spirit in which it is intended, but I think you are being very academic. (Smiles)

Ellen: (Laughs) I am academic!

Elizabeth: My opinion is that the faith-based movement was born out of real needs at the community level. Someone realized that Baptists, Methodists, Jewish congregations, non-denominational groups, etc.–especially in African-American and Latino communities where church is traditionally a respected, trusted authority in the lives of so many–were doing some real heart-changing, soul-changing, life changing ministries–making a lasting difference in people's lives. So to be inclusive, this was an initiative that came out of a spiritual base, a faith base. I think that is all it was ever intended to be, which is what you knew already.

Ellen: But that is helpful. What you said is that it is based in some group . . .

Elizabeth: Based in community whatever that means in local terms–not based upon a particular religious group, but upon serving ministering groups which happen to be spiritual or faith-based in most instances . . . people ministering to others for life-changing results . . . getting people off welfare, helping them toward self sufficiency, not with the intent to convert to a particular religion necessarily. Some of course do have a conversion goal, but that is not what this movement was born out of, although there is that element in some ministries. Charitable Choice, which as you know was first passed in 1996 along with welfare reform, states clearly that government funds may not be used for sectarian worship, instruction or proselytization. Government funding is to be used to provide a service. These other activities can be a part of what is offered but must be voluntary and separately funded.

Jim: I'm curious about the lines between formal and informal service delivery. There were a lot of efforts in the 80s about how we would stimulate more local helpers, folks that were exemplary in the neighborhoods, and what we found is that when we go into an informal situation, it either becomes more formal or you kill it in trying to structure it. So it assumes somewhat of a formality . . .

Elizabeth: Yes, I see what you mean.

Ellen: I teach outcome-based measurement and the problem is that kind of an approach is different than what informal groups do. To try to put the assumptions of outcome-based measurement on top of informal groups, you have to cross paradigms (excuse the academic language!). My basic assumption as an informal system may be that since I have a good heart I will make a difference, performance-based programming is based on assumptions that are completely different from the way folks work in these situations. To put those assumptions on the informal system, we jump paradigms. That is academic in language, but it is real at the local level when you have to implement it, and then you may lose the "value added" that makes faith-based services different.

Elizabeth: And that is very well recognized, I think, in this whole initiative. First of all, we know that there are not a lot of solid data to say that faith-based ministries are more effective because of just that reason. They are just doing it and may not be keeping records of success. They are not saying that they've tracked this mom for 5-10 years and she has held a job, has custody of her children and has remained drug free. What they do know in many cases, since she may still be in the neighborhood, is that she does not come to the soup kitchen any more, the police are not frequently at her door and her children are not running the street at all hours of the night. They know she's better off now than she was when they first intervened. So that's an interesting point. On the government side, another complicating factor is that there is no definition for faith-based, so in many instances we may not even know if a group we are funding classifies themselves as faith-based. That makes it difficult to gather data on the efficacy of some programs. We can't say how many faith-based organizations we are funding. The federal government is very uneasy about defining it and frankly, I am relieved that government is not trying to impose a definition upon groups of faith. We realize now, however, that the success of this initiative will be harder to capture unless we help groups define their status and equally important, that we help them with evaluation of their programs–all government funded programs should be able to prove their effectiveness–not just faith-based programs. We want to be sensitive to the fact that if government, even the faith-based initiative component, asks groups to self-define up front, many won't apply for funding. Some will feel that this information may be a part of what is weighed in their grant application. Regarding this initiative, we would like to look at ministries which are already effectively serving with or without government funding, those who know what it means to have outcome-based measurements or performance measures. We hope some may be willing to mentor a new service provider in the evaluation area. But I agree that there are some groups which, if we superimpose this whole outcome-based model over their ministries, may change what they do in the process that the very thing which makes them effective and unique is compromised as well, and that would be a great loss. Not all groups are good candidates to receive government funding with the necessary audits, evaluations, and reporting requirements that are necessary to ensure some level of accountability. Part of this initiative is also to find ways to help groups build their capacity in management areas so they can compete and they can do so without compromising their mission. They need to know what it is like to manage a contract, to have an audit, to provide quarterly audit reports. We do not have funding in all of our grant programs to provide technical assistance, but it sure is a good idea, especially technical assistance for evaluating the success of a program. I should think that the groups would welcome a good evaluation component rather than see it as intrusive, because if they are not being effective in some areas, then let's not fund that area, let's put those funds to use where they can be more effective–more bang for the buck! Back to your original comment, I do follow the paradigm shift.

Jim: This pattern is important to note. For example, I'm aware of a program through the Presbyterian Church in which a nurse's aide was hired by a congregation using foundation funds to create a parish nurse type program. When it came right down to it what she did was she stopped by and visited 3-4 people in the community and said that she spent x amount of time nursing them. Keep in mind that this was a nurse's aide with six weeks of clinical training. We sat there at the foundation and said there's no program here. What we have is a person doing visiting, but how does that translate into a recognized program. Should the church be doing something like that? Yes, of course, but it makes for a difficult fit as there are formal guidelines for the development of a Parish Nurse Program which generally include Registered Nurses with more training. They also include some type of supervision, both from nursing and from the parish, as well as a formal procedure for identifying clients and the other activities of the parish nurse program. In this case you have an example of an informal service without the supervision, training and administrative support. If our formal programs are the only way that we are defining services, then you are forced to eliminate certain groups such as a congregation that is providing what could be a great service, albeit in a more informal model such as the Presbyterian Church in question.

Elizabeth: I think your use of the term "kind of eliminating certain groups" is interesting because we aren't picking and choosing the groups who participate. We're opening the door and leveling the playing field, doing what we can to facilitate some capacity building. That's a self-selection process to me. If a group is serious about wanting to become engaged, they have a lot of work to do. So, I don't see that we are eliminating them, but they are opting out of the process if they feel it is too burdensome. Now, our main goal is to eliminate unnecessary barriers, make it as easy and user friendly as possible. We should facilitate the efforts of these groups and, where we can, government should get out of their way! The example you gave seems to be from the perspective of a foundation which has a different function in my opinion. In fact HHS funds a variety of programs similar to the one you describe. We see real value in disseminating health-related information to congregations, teaching them good health habits based upon the latest research. It will affect their disease rates, hospitalization, recovery and so on.

Jim: So if you create the structure, then they must buy into it?

Elizabeth: Well, with government funds comes the need for accountability and that is the structure in place. This is taxpayer money! This brings me to yet another important point. Businesses and foundations as well as private charitable donors need to take a much more active role in funding some of these organizations. Community support is paramount to their success. To be a sustaining factor is not the role of government.

Jim: That's really a helpful thing to say–here's government's role and we're not trying to support or not support formal versus informal groups. That recasts the role of your office.

Elizabeth: And I think there's been some confusion about what our role is because we haven't defined it very well. We get a lot of proposals from people who are doing great things or who want to start up a new ministry or program. Generally, it is not our role to evaluate these wonderful programs and to decide whether we are going to fund them or not. Our role, with few exceptions, is to provide the funding opportunity for an identified need, and give any and all the opportunity to respond to that need. We are not in the business of funding all their great projects because there just isn't enough money.

Jim: It's a little bit like going to the gas pump in your car. What you are trying to do is to put a filter on the gas pump. You're not trying to decide what type of car it goes into. (Laughter over the metaphor.)

Elizabeth: (Laughs) I think what I get from the gas pump metaphor is that you want the filter for quality control, but right now, until we get our reforms in place, you can only use unleaded because all the spigots are the same.

Jim: And what your office is trying to do is to take the filters off that say that you can't put it into certain things. On the other hand, what you are not doing is defining the car.

Elizabeth: The filters are important but we don't need to have so many we can't fill the tank! And you are right–we are not defining the car but we are saying it has to have four wheels, it has to run, it has to have an engine . . . we're not going to fund scooters, but four door cars with windows that roll up and that have air-conditioning.

Jim: What message do you have from this position to stimulate that kind of an approach? What you're saying is that it needs to be the local folks who really need to take on some of this stuff. Is there a way for you to push something downstream that would help them?

Elizabeth: That is such a good question. When I look at the federal government from way up here, I see billions of dollars going to the states in the form of block grants and I see a relative trickle going from HHS to individual grantees in the form of discretionary money–money which we can directly influence. Our Center is working to affect change in those discretionary streams by clarifying policies, revising rules and internal guidance to create an environment where more faith-based and community serving groups can participate. It is up to the states to continue these efforts by reviewing their contracting procedures, streamlining their processes and reaching out to nontraditional potential grantees. It is the responsibility of the federal government to let the states know about this new environment, to dispel some of the myths about strict separation, and to encourage state and local governments to look to these new partners as allies in the battle against dependancy and poverty. Government has in many ways traditionally thought that when a group takes federal funds they had to secularize and sanitize any religious elements that made them unique. This has in fact been the expectation in many programs but with this initiative dawns a new day where groups can remain true to their mission under Charitable Choice. Our goal is to clarify the principles that now guide relationships between government and faith-based service providers. I keep using Texas because it's what I know best. In Texas, through our Department of Human Services we pulled Charitable Choice language from the bill and we put it up front in all of our contracts, in our RFP, and we didn't have to do that. But we made the statement and then we designated liaisons in all regions of the state. Then we created a tool that took a year to create, in both English and Spanish, and it was built on Dr. Sherman's Handbook for Ministry Leaders. So that when Temple Beth El or when Ebenezer Baptist Church came to the DHS office and said that we want to do something, we knew how to walk them through the process. And it is labor intensive, but I think it takes all of those layers all the way down in order to effect change. At the same time we are also reaching out to national religious organizations of all flavors. We'll be speaking there, we'll be providing materials to let them know what the initiative is about and what some of the opportunities are, and what we don't do. So I think it is going to take a whole lot of elements in order to actually make a difference in the local area.

Ellen: This just reminded me of the concept of bureaucratic disentitlement coined by Michael Lipsky. It relates to what happens at the local level when line workers perform their jobs in a way that disentitles recipients of service. It occurs to me that if local workers interpret the separation of church and state in certain ways, it becomes true, whether it is or not. Soon that becomes part of the practice. What you are saying is that there are assumptions about what should not be allowed that appear to be part of established practice but are not required by law.

Elizabeth: That's great, and I'm going to use that concept. Let me give you another example and you'll find this in the report that I'll give you. In the abstinence-based programs that started in the 80s, many faith-based organizations naturally applied for funding. There was a court case that went all of the way to the Supreme Court, the Supreme Court remanded it back to the state, and there was an out-of-court settlement. But the out-of-court settlement, *Bone versus Kendrick*, was very prescriptive to grantees and, boy, did they have to secularize. They had to show all of their curriculum; they couldn't have icons; they couldn't do this, this, this and this. Well, that was a court case and you have to do what you are told. That expired in 1998 after five years. Well, you know what we found. We found that we are still using that for internal guidance with the full knowledge that this is expired. And, in not only that, but it has bled over into two or three other programs. Grantees have to fill out this 13-page questionnaire on how religious or not religious they are. So up front in those new grant applications or in letters to grantees, or however we work with that program, we'll be letting them know that this is not the case any more. And the program area will work with us and we'll talk back and forth about what's the best way to get the information down to the grantee level. So, those kinds of things completely describe what you are saying.

Jim: Then let me invite you to the next annual meeting of the National Interfaith Coalition on Aging and the Forum on Religion, Spirituality and Aging. I think they need to hear your message and it might allow for a forum of exchange between representatives of some of the national religious bodies as well as individual workers in the field.

Elizabeth: If you think that anything I've said would be helpful to them, I'd be glad to meet with them.

Jim: Yes, to whatever extent we can figure out where the channels are, and in some ways it is important to say that maybe we don't have any more money but this is how we can make a connection. This is how we can increase a skill here.

Elizabeth: We'd just be delighted to participate. And hasn't it just been in the last little bit that aging has become a more common topic of discussion to be looked at more carefully with new Alzheimer's projects, studies related to suicide rates, depression and the elderly, the need to connect in a more meaningful way with our older Americans to enhance their health and quality of life? Maybe it's just my age that's brought me to the point, but we seem to be talking about it more.

Jim: You are right. In comparison to other disciplines like Sociology or Psychology, Gerontology is much newer. Indeed, the inclusion of religion and spirituality is even newer. The field of gerontology dates back to the late 1940s with the initiation of the Gerontological Society of America. Ironically, the various White

House Conferences reflect the growth of the inclusion of religious groups and spiritual concerns into the field. In the 1951 and 1961 White House Conferences, there were sections on the topic of religion. The 1961 conference papers were the first to be fully developed. Written by Paul Maves, these documents are often used as examples of the initiation of religious concerns into Gerontology. While other, previous projects and documents exist, Paul's work offered a beginning focus for future projects. In 1971, there was a feeling among the organizers of the White House Conference on Aging that religion was not a broad enough term to be fully inclusive. Thus a new term, Spiritual Well-being, was proposed by Clark Tibbits and his staff. The term seems to have grown out of the then-accepted term psychological well-being. The term was field tested by Grover Hartman in a conference in Indiana with much success, and thus adopted as the new section in the White House Conference. Paul Maves was once again asked to develop the papers for this section; however, he turned this assignment down as he was in transition to St. Paul School of Theology in Kansas City. David O. Moberg did an excellent job of developing these documents and has since that time played a visible role in the ongoing development of the field. Out of the 1971 White House Conference, David Moberg, Don Clingan, Tom Cooke and others developed the National Interfaith Coalition on Aging in order to orchestrate a response to the work of the 1971 White House Conference. This task has been central to the work of this group ever since, and has continued since the merger between the National Interfaith Coalition on Aging and the National Council on the Aging. The White House Conferences in the 1980s and 1990s offered very little support for religion or spiritual well-being. During this time, however, the concept of spirituality, was promoted by many in the field and became an important part of the development of the new group, the Forum on Religion, Spirituality and Aging, a constituent unit of the American Society on Aging. So the terms in this field have changed. The term Spiritual Well-being actually has two definitions. The first is the one developed by the National-Interfaith Coalition on Aging. Their definition is as follows: "Spiritual Well-Being is the affirmation of life in a relationship with God, self, community, and environment that nurtures and celebrates wholeness."[1] The second definition does not enjoy the same type of agreement among scholars, but many of those who are trying to employ this term in research often use a definition that more closely resembles the origin of the term to reflect measures of spiritual happiness. The term spiritual by itself has a long history of definition by theologians, but has not achieved any sort of agreement by researchers. Do you have a working definition you are using for the terms spirituality or spiritual well-being?

Elizabeth: No. Across government there is not one nor one that I can say is definitive even within HHS programs.

Jim: There is not one definition of religion either. Theologians can give you a very concrete definition. Sociologists can also define this term, as it tends to refer to the operation of formal groups.

Ellen: As you were talking, you also jump to another set of assumptions and that is the empowerment of the individual as opposed to the empowerment of the community. Spirituality in the transpersonal use of the word, is highly individualistic. I think there is a difference between the concept of spirituality as it is being used by social workers and the concept of groups whose spirituality is centered in organized religion. So, it seems we are using the term all over the place and the language is not precise. The language keeps us from communicating the intent of where we want to go. The spirituality literature is everywhere these days but I don't see it as interfacing with the concepts we have been discussing here.

Jim: There are two journals in the field of social work which attempt to bring religious and spiritual issues together with social service practice. The *Journal of Religion in the Social Services* is edited by the faculty of the School of Social Services at Catholic University. This journal has a historic tie with Catholic Charities, but is currently produced by the Haworth Press. There is also the *Journal of Christianity and Social Work* produced by the North American Association of Christians in Social Work. In much of the social work literature, the preferred definitions of religion and spirituality have been more inclusive of world religions.

Elizabeth: You have given me some food for thought, not that I have any time to think about it! (Laughs) The question for me personally comes down to this: how do you give that welfare mother the choice to use a faith-based provider, let's say, for her job training program? A ministry like Lutheran Social Services, for example, is generally in the business because they have the time to mentor her for eight months, if that is what she needs and the time to help her make decisions which will deeply affect her life choices, her family, her health–they may or may not use the Bible as a basic tool for guidance to help her in her decision-making process but the principles used have a spiritual basis: responsibility, accountability, dependability, etc., and that kind of interaction in a person's life is empowering! Government is less suited to nurture these life changing one-on-one interpersonal relationships. Now the question becomes how do we engage people in this process in a corporate sense. Individuals can go out as volunteers, but if you want to enable the armies of compassion, as the President says, then this type of help needs to be replicated many times over within the private sector.

Jim: Historically it is clear in the literature that religion separates community groups into denominational groups. The term spirituality, on the other hand, is more likely to bond them together. One of the lessons that was learned by the National Interfaith Coalition on Aging as they sought to bring together the various denominations to work on behalf of older adults is that diverse religious groups are more likely to come together around their common ministries with older adults, than around either the terms religion or spirituality.

Elizabeth: You may have some ideas on that, much more than I. The door is open, wide open. I am in agreement with your comment that religion separates and spirituality bonds together. This initiative seeks to lessen the restraints on spiritual healers and helpers in a positive sense to the benefit of those in need.

Question added in December, 2001.

Jim: Since we last spoke, the events of September 11 have made many changes in government. Have there been any changes in the Center for Faith-Based and Community Initiatives?

Elizabeth: Since we last spoke we have had the privilege of being asked to represent the faith community in the mental health response to the tragedies of September 11th. At the request of HHS

Secretary Tommy Thompson, the Center for Faith-Based and Community Initiatives worked with the Substance Abuse and Mental Health Services Administration (SAMHSA) to put on a national summit regarding the mental health issues of the nation in the aftermath of 9/11. There has been increased frustration voiced by the faith community, both local and national, regarding the difficulty in securing a coordinated, meaningful place of service in the response efforts. The conference's faith-based plenary, workshop, and roundtable helped participants to better appreciate both the short-term and long-term importance of partnering with local and national spiritual representatives in an effort to provide the most comprehensive and appropriate care for affected individuals in times of crisis. In addition, participants in the faith-based workshop and roundtable identified issues, solutions, and recommendations regarding the appropriate role of the faith community in disaster response. It is significant to note that this represents a new understanding by the federal government of the importance of spiritual care in times of crisis.

NOTE

1. Thorson, James W. and Thomas C. Cook, Jr. (Eds.) *Spiritual Well-Being of the Elderly* (Springfield: Charles C Thomas Publisher, 1980). xiii.

Baptist Perspectives on Faith-Based Initiatives and Religious Liberty

Jon Singletary, PhD, MSW, MDiv

SUMMARY. Baptist perspectives are presented on recent policy efforts that could increase the opportunities for religious organizations to receive public monies for the planning and delivery of human services. A distinctive Baptist principle is religious liberty, a tenet of faith that contributes to several Baptist writings that consider the risks of church-state relationships in human service activities. Political and philosophical perspectives are considered in a discussion of services that Baptists provide and an understanding of these services as faith-based initiatives. The ElderCare Program of Buckner Baptist Benevolences in Texas and other services are discussed as models of faith-based initiatives for older adults. *[Article copies available for a fee from The Haworth Document Delivery Service:*

Jon Singletary is Assistant Professor, School of Social Work, Baylor University, Waco, Texas.

The author would like to express his appreciation to Buckner Baptist Benevolences in Texas for the information on the Eldercare Program and other Baptist human services for older adults. Mary Stephens, Vice President of Buckner Retirement Services; Charlie Wilson, Director of Quality Improvement and Regulatory Compliance for Buckner Retirement Services; and social work administrators from around the state including Charles Childress, Sandra Johnson, and Karen Havens were particularly helpful in providing literature, resources, and comments in helping him understand Buckner programs. His grandfather-in-law, Sidney Reber, supplied valuable materials on Texas Baptists' perspectives on Faith-Based Initiatives and an example of faith-based leadership.

[Haworth co-indexing entry note]: "Baptist Perspectives on Faith-Based Initiatives and Religious Liberty." Singletary, Jon. Co-published simultaneously in *Journal of Religious Gerontology* (The Haworth Pastoral Press, an imprint of The Haworth Press, Inc.) Vol. 16, No. 1/2, 2004, pp. 81-98; and: *Faith-Based Initiatives and Aging Services* (ed: F. Ellen Netting, and James W. Ellor) The Haworth Pastoral Press, an imprint of The Haworth Press, Inc., 2004, pp. 81-98. Single or multiple copies of this article are available for a fee from The Haworth Document Delivery Service [1-800-HAWORTH, 9:00 a.m. - 5:00 p.m. (EST). E-mail address: docdelivery@haworthpress.com].

http://www.haworthpress.com/web/JRG
Digital Object Identifier: 10.1300/J078v16n01_05

1-800-HAWORTH. E-mail address: <docdelivery@haworthpress.com> Website: <http://www.HaworthPress.com> © 2004 by The Haworth Press, Inc. All rights reserved.]

KEYWORDS. Faith-Based Initiatives, Baptists, religious liberty, church-state

The term "faith-based initiatives" can refer to the policy efforts introduced by President George W. Bush that seek to expand the charitable choice provisions of the 1996 Welfare Reform Act, but the term can also refer to the human service activities of religious organizations.[1] In discussions of faith-based initiatives as public policies, the goal is to remove the barriers to government funding of faith-based human services. Faith-based initiatives, described as the human service efforts of religious organizations and congregations to meet the needs of people in their local communities, include activities in which many religious groups have been involved throughout history.

This article presents the involvement of Baptists in faith-based initiatives both through responses to recent policy efforts and through planning and delivering services to people in need. By discussing issues of religious liberty, such as the separation of church and state, I identify an historical Baptist distinctive that contributes to the public discourse on faith-based initiatives. I include several Baptist perspectives on charitable choice and the legislation introduced into Congress that would reduce barriers to the federal funding of religious human service activities. I also introduce Baptist organizations that provide human services as well as issues related to the federal funding of these services. Comments from two directors of Baptist organizations demonstrate their efforts in the delivery of faith-based human services as well as their understanding of how federal funding for services affects religious liberty. Finally, I provide examples of Baptist programs for older adults in Texas, discussing these programs as examples of faith-based initiatives.

RELIGIOUS LIBERTY AS A BAPTIST DISTINCTIVE

At the dawn of the twenty-first century Baptists prepare to celebrate their 400th birthday with church members numbering over 40 million people in more than 200 countries in every continent of the world (Shurden, 2001, p.1). Overcoming their beginnings of persecution and exile in the seventeenth century, Baptists have not only grown in size to become the largest single Protestant denomination in the United States, but have also maintained their historical distinctive elements such as an emphasis on biblical authority, a church comprised of adult believers, and the goal of equality for each believing individual in the church (Anderson, 1995). In the unity of this heritage, there is also increasing diversity among the dozens of different Baptist bodies in the United States. The religious liberty that yields a creative tension between unity and diversity has long been identified as a major identifying characteristic of Baptists. In fact, religious liberty is described as the greatest gift that Baptists have offered to the character of religious life in the United States (Goodwin, 1997).

In presenting Baptist perspectives on faith-based initiatives, it is helpful to note that Baptist discussions of these issues focus largely on matters of religious liberty, with an emphasis on understanding the appropriate measure of separation between church and state. Stan Hastey (1979) distinguishes between religious liberty and the separation of church and state describing the terms not as twins, but close relatives. He describes religious liberty as "a theological concept rooted in Scripture. Separation of church and state is the method devised by the nation's founders to implement the principle of religious liberty" (p. 1). Baptists helped to secure the separation of church and state early in the history of the United States because of the religious liberty they believed God had granted to all people (Hastey, 1979).

"To be a Baptist is to believe in religious freedom," William Estep (1989, p. 1) writes for the Historical Commission of the Southern Baptist Convention. Baptists in the United States are a diverse body of evangelical Christians that value biblical authority and regenerate church membership, yet soul freedom and the separation of church and state derive from their foremost guiding principle, that of religious liberty. Issues to be discerned in considering Baptist perspectives on faith-based initiatives must take into account these distinctive elements of Baptist heritage.

In seeking to balance evangelical and human service goals, Baptists value faith-based services and offer many examples of their own. Kenneth Hall (2001), President of Buckner Baptist Benevolences in Texas, contributes to the Baptist consideration of faith-based initiatives by offering a distinction between what he believes to be philosophical and real world perspectives on the issue. While I do not depend on his understanding of what is philosophical and what is real, I will utilize this typology to organize my account of Baptist perspectives on faith-based initiatives. I present historical Baptist principles, issues that can be identified as philosophical ideas, and then, examples of real world Baptist efforts. Philosophical perspectives are focused on Baptist understandings of religious liberty. The real world perspectives will include comments from Baptist leaders on how religious liberty may shape faith-based programs and program funding, using examples of Baptist programs for both children and older adults.

AN HISTORICAL OVERVIEW OF BAPTISTS AND RELIGIOUS LIBERTY

Baptists were born in 1609, coming out of the English Reformation. John Smyth and Thomas Helwys, leaders in the Church of England, attempted to restore the church, but eventually formed a group of Separatists. They later became known as a distinct group, the Baptists, who emphasized the baptism of adults and claimed salvation in Jesus Christ. In what was seen by many as a scandalous act, Smyth baptized himself, Helwys and others in their congregation in criticism of infant baptism and in affirmation of freedom and equality among Christians (McBeth, 1987; Torbet, 1963).

In the seventeenth and eighteenth centuries, Baptists experienced restrictions placed upon them by government-controlled churches. They insisted upon their belief that the state should not interfere with their religious practices and that the church will not look to the state for financial support. One of the first contributors to this ideal of freedom in the New World of the Americas was Roger Williams, who was a Baptist for only a short period of time. His contribution to religious freedom in the early days of American life forged a distinctive that has shaped long-standing Baptist perspectives on church-state issues and recent Baptist views on faith-based initiatives. Baptist beliefs concerning religious liberty vary from congregation to congregation, and more importantly to Baptists, from individual to individual, but across these viewpoints, Baptists will refer to the founding efforts of Williams, and the similar influence of other Baptist leaders such as Isaac Backus and John Leland. Together, these three Baptist leaders have shaped not only Baptist perspectives on faith-based initiatives, but also the broader national dialogue emphasizing faith-based initiatives as complex issues of church and state.

In 1636, Roger Williams was forced to flee the Massachusetts Bay Colony because of his teachings on "soul liberty." Williams was baptized as an adult in 1639, proclaiming the value of adult religious conversions and rejecting infant baptisms. He founded the Rhode Island colony in 1636, and in 1639 founded the first Baptist church in the New World. These new "state" and "church" institutions guaranteed freedom from one another, and proclaimed the value of religious liberty (McBeth, 1987). Williams appreciated a Baptist view of the church, and although he moved to another religious group, he maintained a Baptist view of keeping political and religious institutions distinct from one another (Torbet, 1963).

A century later, in the era of the American Revolution, Isaac Backus continued a Baptist focus on issues of religious liberty. Backus was a leader in the Rhode Island Warren Association, formed for the purpose of influencing the Continental Congress in Philadelphia to provide a guarantee of absolute religious liberty (Torbet, 1963). Backus traveled throughout the colonies, visiting churches and rallying Baptists to the cause of liberty, continually proclaiming that state tyranny would come with state control of churches.

John Leland was another spokesperson for religious freedom in this era. The Anglican Church in Virginia resented the presence of Baptists and as their persecution increased, Leland added an emphasis on the role of freedom of personal conscience to his revival sermons on faith and grace. In letters, statements, and sermons, he worked with the General Committee of Baptists in Virginia, arguing that governments should let all persons be free in terms of religious matters. He worked to shape the thought of James Madison and Thomas Jefferson, with the result being a statement of religious liberty passed by the Virginia General Assembly in 1785, and the First Amendment of the Bill of Rights in the federal Constitution in 1791. From their beginnings through the shaping of the United States Bill of Rights, Baptists were involved in efforts to promote religious liberty.

PHILOSOPHICAL PERSPECTIVES OF BAPTISTS INVOLVED TO PROMOTE RELIGIOUS LIBERTY

Baptists did not again emphasize as strongly the subject of religious liberty until the twentieth century. The work of Baptists in the nineteenth century focused more on evangelical mission efforts and on issues of slavery which divided Baptists of the North and the South. Out of a commitment to the role of religious liberty in Baptist heritage, a group of Baptists from the North and South, both black and white, met in Washington, D.C. in the late 1930s to monitor developments affecting religious practices throughout the country. The group became known as the Baptist Joint Committee on Public Affairs (BJC), an organization that has maintained its commitment to educating and shaping political and religious leadership to remain aware of matters related to religious liberty and to promote the separation of church and state.

In the 1990s, Baptists have had opportunities to emphasize again the role of religious liberty with the introduction of charitable choice legislation and other faith-based policy initiatives. The BJC along with other Baptist groups, including the Baptist General Convention of Texas Christian Life Commission, and even the more conservative Southern Baptist Ethics and Religious Liberty Commission, have been vocal in criticizing faith-based initiatives as unconstitutional policies that encroach upon religious liberties, break down the wall between separation of church and state, and lead to a state establishment of religious practice.

Melissa Rogers (1999), Executive Director of the Pew Forum on Religion and Public Life and former general counsel at the BJC, suggests several negative implications of the federal funding of faith-based services: these policy initiatives advance religion in ways that violate the U.S. Constitution, create unhealthy competition among religious organizations for limited government grants and contracts, enmesh religion in the political appropriations process, transform ministries into government-related administrative centers, undermine the prophetic voice of religion, make religious efforts dependent on tax money and beholden to the government, expose religious organizations to government policies and regulations, and sanction government-funded religious discrimination in employment.

Brent Walker (2001), Executive Director of the BJC, states his opposition to federal funding of faith-based services in a statement similar to that of Rogers. He writes that policies to fund faith-based services with government money, such as charitable choice, threaten to promote religion in a way that violates the Establishment Clause of the First Amendment, entangle churches in government policies and regulations, dampen the prophetic voice of religion, endorse employment discrimination on the basis of religion, and encourage unhealthful rivalry for a limited amount of money.

According to Walker, the problem with charitable choice is not the end goal of delivering faith-based social services, but the political means by which religious programs are at risk of becoming beholden to government control. He states that Baptists should oppose government funding of religious services because of a desire "to keep those faith-based services vital and free" (Walker, 2001, p. 3).

In the same issue of *Report from the Capital*, Derek Davis (2001), director of the Dawson Institute of Church-State Studies at Baylor University, expresses concern that faith-based initiatives risk "just being thought of by the American people as another government program." He describes recent policy initiatives as the "right motive, wrong method" (Davis, 2001, p. 1). Walker (2001) concurs and offers better ways to do right. He encourages private giving that would allow congregations to offer services with tithes, offerings, and other private sources. He recommends that congregations that might benefit from more formal organizational efforts create separate nonprofit organizations to accept government funding for their social services. These organizations would maintain the faith-based motivation but without entangling the federal funds and policies into those of the congregation, and with protections that prevent proselytization, discrimination, and the teaching of religion from being a part of the human services offered. Walker also supports creative non-financial cooperation between religion and government. Sharing information, fostering volunteer and service opportunities, and making referrals allow government and congregations to work toward similar goals in an integral process that ensures the autonomy of congregations and protects the religious liberty of all persons involved in the process of service delivery.

The Baptist Joint Committee is supported by fourteen of the nation's Baptist bodies, which accounts for a large segment of Baptists in the United States. The largest Baptist body, and the largest protestant denomination in the United States, the Southern Baptist Convention, parted ways with the BJC when fundamentalist leadership came to power in the early 1980s. The Southern Baptist Ethics and Religious Liberty Commission (ERLC) serves as their more conservative voice on moral and political issues, but director Richard Land voiced a similar Baptist opposition to faith-based initiatives stating that he "wouldn't touch this with a ten foot pole" ("SBC leader," 2001, p. 6). After Land attended a Faith-Based Summit sponsored by Republican congressional leadership, ERLC press statements quoted Land as saying, "there are ways to do this that will pass constitutional muster and be acceptable" (Strode, 2001a, p. 1). Land's leadership of the ERLC is often accused of making Southern Baptists into a partisan body by supporting Republican efforts, but he has been firm in demanding that faith-based initiatives must meet certain ground rules if they are going to be constitutional and successful. Land states that government aid go only to the non-faith-based phases of the program with congregations privately funding religious aspects. He also suggests that viable secular alternatives be available to recipients of human services and that no religious group be discriminated against in the distribution of funds. While not endorsing faith-based policies, Land now says he is more assured that faith-based services can be empowered by the initiatives ("SBC leader," 2001; Strode, 2001b).

Keeping the Faith, a document recently published by the BJC together with the Interfaith Alliance states Baptist perspectives on faith-based initiatives most clearly and concisely. This document describes possibilities for religion and government cooperation, poses questions for religious organizations, and provides helpful illustrations of positive and negative relationships that preserve the religious liberty of organizations. The document presents negative implications for government funding of religious activities. It also includes appendices with suggestions for non-financial cooperation between religion and government, and private sources for funding religious human services.

At a press conference organized by diverse religious leaders to foster religious liberty and oppose President Bush's Faith-Based bill in Congress (H.R. 7), Welton Gaddy (2001), Baptist pastor and director of the Interfaith Alliance, commented that this legislation would create a social services system that would be able to discriminate, coerce and proselytize in the name of religion. He asked several guiding questions showing that the initiative is "short on compassion, and long on problems" (Gaddy, 2001, pp. 1-2): Where is the compassion in creating a system where those in need must choose between receiving services and maintaining their civil and religious rights? Where is the constitutional integrity in a religiously diverse nation picking and choosing which religions to fund and which to exclude? Where is the social justice in allowing religious institutions to use government funds to discriminate on the basis of religion? Where is the compassion in employing religious institutions to enforce government deadlines and restrictions on the most vulnerable?

The challenges presented by these Baptist leaders and by the organizations they represent cover legal, practical, organizational, and ethical implications relevant to congregations, other organizations delivering services, and individuals receiving services. Guided by traditions of religious liberty, these Baptists support the delivery of faith-based social services, but they want to make sure the services are not restricted by government policies and procedures; they also strive to make sure the individuals receiving services are not forced to participate in religious practices.

A unique Baptist contribution to Protestantism, and the world, is a consistent witness to the principle of religious liberty (Torbet, 1963). Many issues are being discussed as positive and negative implications of charitable choice and other faith-based initiatives, and Baptists have been consistent in their contribution to the policy debate. If through these initiatives, government has the potential to advance, transform, undermine, make dependent, or control religion, or in any way remove a protective wall that separates church and state, then a Baptist presence can be heard to raise the awareness of religious liberties at risk. In showing the breadth of their concerns and in continuing their unique contribution, Baptists involved in service delivery have also commented on matters relating to religious liberty and faith-based initiatives.

PRACTICAL PERSPECTIVES OF BAPTISTS PROVIDING FAITH-BASED SERVICES

Some Baptist voices can be heard promoting religious liberty by criticizing charitable choice, and others are expressing opportunities to put their faith in action without being concerned about government interference. In looking at Baptist involvement in the planning and delivery of faith-based human service initiatives, I will limit my focus to a discussion of programs offered in association with one state level Baptist organization, the Baptist General Convention of Texas (BGCT). The BGCT largely depends on the efforts of local Baptist agencies and congregations that carry out their ministries by offering a variety of human service programs. The BGCT utilizes several affiliated human service organizations to plan and deliver service programs.

Programs affiliated with the BGCT provide Baptist examples of faith-based human service initiatives. This review of Baptist programs in Texas demonstrates only one approach to understanding Baptist perspectives on the subject, but these perspectives reflect traditional Baptist approaches to church-state relationships and to offering human services. The Human Care Ministry Website of the BGCT (2001) describes how the organization understands their Baptist commitment to "the mission of the human welfare institutions to extend the love of Christ to people in need." The BGCT is recognized for its commitment to historic Baptist principles and to caring for humans in need, making this organization a valuable example of Baptist involvement in faith-based human service programs.

ISSUES RAISED
BY TEXAS BAPTIST CHILD WELFARE AGENCIES

There are four childcare organizations affiliated with the BGCT that are part of Texas Baptist human service efforts, each with sites of ministry all over the state. These include Buckner Children and Family Services, Dallas Baptist Child and Family Services, South Texas Children's Home, and Texas Baptist Children's Home. The discussion here is limited to Buckner Children and Family Services and South Texas Children's Home. While only one of these organizations utilizes federal funds for their ministries, both are relevant to current policy discussions as they can be described in terms of the faith that provides a basis for their programs.

Discussions about faith-based initiatives led the presidents of two Texas Baptist organizations to submit opinion articles to the *Baptist Standard*, the state newspaper of Texas Baptists. Kenneth Hall (2001), President of Buckner Baptist Benevolences, offers the distinction utilized in this paper regarding the two worlds of the faith-based funding debate. His "real world perspective" comes from the practices of "faith-based child-care agencies," such as the organization he serves. Jerry Haag (2001), President of South Texas Children's Home, provides several important questions that have shaped their decision to refuse state and federal funds.

Buckner is one of the largest private social-care ministries in the nation, serving approximately 40,000 people each year. The organization is governed by a 27-member Board of Trustees, which is elected by the Baptist General Convention of Texas. Buckner receives funding from diverse sources including 2 percent from the BGCT. A majority of the revenues come from client support and related income (58 percent) and real estate sales and investment income (26 percent). Contributions make up 11 percent of funding, and public money for contracted services contributes less than 1 percent to Buckner revenues (Buckner Baptist Benevolences Annual Report, 2001).

South Texas Children's Home (STCH) also receives funding from the BGCT, but does not enter into state or federal government contracts and does not accept government funds for operation. This affiliate organization of the BGCT receives approximately 30% of its annual budget from the convention and describes itself as a debt-free organization. A board of 24 directors also elected by the Baptist General Convention of Texas governs STCH (STCH, 2001). Both STCH and Buckner offer programs fully licensed by the state of Texas and regularly serve children placed by Child Protective Services.

The comments of presidents Hall and Haag offer differing practical perspectives of Texas Baptists on the issues of faith-based initiatives. Hall feels that if "Caesar wants to give to God" as is the case in the funding of religiously affiliated child-care agencies, hospitals, and colleges and universities, and if the funding doesn't restrict the mission of the agency, then the real beneficiaries are the people served by the programs offered. If the funding assures that the religious beliefs of each person involved are protected, then Hall believes Baptists should be supportive of the funding opportunity. Hall is clear in his belief that organizations can utilize federal funding without hindering religious freedoms. He states that Baptists, who should always be advocates for religious liberty, "have the opportunity at this point in the faith-based initiatives program to ensure that the religious beliefs of every person are protected, even if those happen to be beliefs with which we do not agree" (Hall, 2001, p. 6). Hall promotes charitable choice and faith-based initiatives while insisting that Baptists should be involved in the discussion at the outset to promote religious freedom.

Haag agrees that Christian ministry and effective faith-based programs can be provided with state and federal monies, but he also believes that government funds will drive the direction of the ministry. He cites government inconsistency in funding social services and the loss of the civil rights exception for hiring in religious organizations that comes with the use of federal funds. Haag comments on the challenges of operating without accessing public money, but believes this is the decision that allows his organization the greatest amount of liberty in their religious practices.

Opportunities for Texas Baptist Senior Adult Agencies

The Baptist General Convention of Texas has shown a commitment to caring for aging Americans. The BGCT Human Care Ministry Website (2001) states that with the "graying of America has come a need to minister to the aging." As a result several Texas Baptist human service organizations provide aging care ministries along with their other areas of care. Programs for senior adults constitute the primary purpose of three organizations sponsored by the BGCT: Baptist Community Services in Amarillo, Baptist Memorials Ministries in San Angelo, and Buckner Retirement Services, Inc. in Dallas. I will briefly describe the programs offered in the Buckner Retirement Services continuum of care and then focus on the ElderCare Program, a Baptist program that can be identified as a genuine faith-based initiative.

The Programs of Buckner Retirement Services

The mission statement of Buckner Retirement Services, Inc. says that "care" has been at the heart of Buckner programs for their duration of their fifty years of service, and that they are "committed to ensuring that each person is treated with dignity and respect" (Buckner Retirement Services, 2001). Buckner offers a continuum of care designed to provide services for different stages of retirement, with a focus on the living environment of senior adults. The Continuum of Care includes the following stages:

ElderCare Services designed for senior adults who choose to stay at home, with services such as home safety assessments, information and referral, wellness checks, and assistance with light household chores, and spiritual support through chaplaincy services.

Independent Living offering a secure living environment in accommodations that include cottages, duplexes, patio homes, or apartments, each with maintenance and scheduled activities.

Assisted Living provided by a professionally trained staff available all day, and with scheduled activities, meals and snacks, transportation, housekeeping, and laundry services.

Nursing Care offered by skilled providers for residents with varying levels of medical needs and services such as meals, housekeeping, laundry, scheduled activities, 24-hour licensed nursing care and a variety of therapeutic services.

The Harbor is designed specifically for individuals with memory loss disorders who are no longer able to live alone, but who may not yet need nursing care; meals, housekeeping, therapeutic activities and other services are also available as needed.

In 2000, 1100 senior adults lived in the different levels of retirement communities offered by Buckner in five locations: Longview, Houston,

Austin, Dallas, and for the first year in Beaumont. Approximately 2000 adults participated in the ElderCare program last year.

The ElderCare Program is a benevolent arm of Buckner Retirement Services that aligns volunteer caregivers with people in different communities across Texas. The program is a model of faith-based service that incorporates a variety of volunteers with opportunities for caregiving in ways that protect the dignity, independence, and general well-being of older adults. While these adults may need support, their desire is to remain in their own homes. Assessment and planning are components of the program that help determine the best solutions or home modifications in efforts to meet the individual needs of seniors. Home safety assessments and geriatric care assessment and referral are also available. The ElderCare program helps to establish personal relationships for senior adults, provides needed services to maintain safety and independence, and as an entry point in the continuum of care, the program introduces senior adults to alternative opportunities for Independent Living, to Assisted Living programs, to Nursing Care, and the Harbor program.

The program has a Senior Care Services component that provides elements such as wellness checks, telephone reassurance, and friendly visitors (Buckner ElderCare, 2001b). The volunteers and other caregivers have knowledge of local resources, options, and services in an effort to assure practical, cost-effective and comfortable solutions to various problems facing older adults. As tasks become more difficult for adults, volunteers are able to provide assistance with tasks such as replacing filters and light bulbs, grocery shopping, and light housekeeping.

Another component of the program is a listing of care providers, a Caregiver Registry, that helps senior adults to choose non-medical care providers of services that go beyond the scope of volunteers and that help senior adults to function safely and adequately in their own homes (Buckner ElderCare, 2001b). Screening of all providers through personal interviews, criminal history and background checks helps to assure competence and security for the adults in the program. Buckner Retirement Services is not the employer of the caregivers, but rather they are privately hired service providers.

The Caregiver Registry process includes materials that help older adults and their family members to discuss services for which caregivers would be helpful. Issues of clarity and decision-making are among items for discussion that are encouraged in order to reduce unrealistic and frustrating expectations. Other discussion items include payment, hours of work, scheduling, emergency services, and overnight care. The Buckner ElderCare Program is helpful since hiring through the registry helps to reduce costs, provides consistency of the caregiver that is hired, includes background screening, a 45-day satisfaction guarantee, additional services such as chaplaincy care, and an in-home assessment of personal needs by a Buckner ElderCare social worker. A "description of relationship" agreement describes the details of the services to be provided by the caregiver to the client.

Additionally, ElderCare is described as a comprehensive ministry that is designed to equip and enable families and churches to meet the needs of aging adults within their congregations and across their communities (Buckner ElderCare, 2001a). Congregations play an important role in the work of the ElderCare program by encouraging senior adults who may benefit from the program to be participants, and by providing volunteers to the program. First Baptist Church of Nacogdoches was the home of this city's ElderCare program in 1997. Program operations began in this church and the church continues to be involved through providing volunteers and through senior adults who are served by the program. The Helen Strahan Thrash Trust that provided initial funding for the program was established in memory of Helen Thrash, an active member of the First Baptist Church of Nacogdoches who wished to turn her home into a boarding house for senior adults. Her sister created the Trust fund to honor her beliefs, values, and commitment to faith-based services for senior adults. This example shows that the time and money of volunteers from local congregations help to make this Buckner program the successful faith-based initiative that it is.

As Baptist faith-based initiatives, the programs of Buckner Retirement Services are rooted in Christian ethical principles, including religious liberty. The ElderCare program is "dedicated to fostering independence and quality of life in aging adults by ministering to their physical, emotional and spiritual needs within the framework of sound Christian principles and professional ethics" (Buckner ElderCare, 2001a, p. 1). While the Christian faith of Baptists is at the heart of Buckner services, the ElderCare program is true to a Baptist concern for religious liberty as services are provided to members of all faiths. The program respects the denominational affiliation and beliefs of all of its clients and will refer any spiritual needs identified by a client to ministers or churches of the client's preference. The public relations and marketing materials make this claim and the staff affirms this commitment, a commitment that makes the program a model faith-based initiative and a model Baptist program because of the way faith shapes the program mission and because the faith of the client is respected (Buckner Eldercare flyer, 2001b).

While public grants and contracts are not currently used for a program such as Buckner's ElderCare, the elements of faith described above are rooted in the program in ways that may make it a model of the faith-based human services lauded by President Bush. If federal grant money were available, the administration at Buckner Retirement Services recognizes that several matters would have to be weighed before they would enter this type of public-private partnership. Unlike Buckner Children and Family Services, Buckner Retirement Services does not access public grants or purchase of service contracts. They do, however, benefit from another form of federal-funding for faith-based services, third party payments connected with Medicare and Medicaid programs. Administrators at Buckner know the benefits as well as the burdens of government and insurance regulations associated with Medicaid and Medicare payments, and as a result, increased options for federal funding are recognized as both opportunity and risk. Buckner administrators feel that as a religiously affiliated organization, their organization may be able to manage the ambiguity and complexity of public-private partnerships better than congregations, but some of them feel that such partnerships might highlight the negative aspects of further breaking down the wall between church and state.

CONCLUSION

Baptists have been protectors of religious liberty and advocates for the separation of church and state throughout their history. Baptists comprise a diverse and sizable body of Christians in the United States, and while many Baptists have been clearly expressing concerns over charitable choice and federal funding of faith-based programs, those who plan and deliver human services are more ambiguous in their perspectives. As practitioners they voice ambivalence about public-private partnerships. The leaders of some human service programs offered by Buckner Baptist Benevolences in Texas recognize the value of the support they receive from local, state and federal governments, whether through grants, purchased services, or third party payments. Other leaders are less confident of the value of these church-state relations as they seek to protect religious liberty recognizing that other liberties are occasionally sacrificed to government regulations.

While there may be some ambivalence concerning matters of funding, Texas Baptists have a clear vision of providing care to older adults. Buckner Retirement Services have been the focus here, but there are other examples of Texas Baptists caring for seniors. Baptist Memorials Ministries in San Angelo dedicated its Sagecrest Alzheimer's Care Center this year; the residential center utilizes a social model of care for people at different stages of Alzheimer's Disease or dementia (Foster, 2001). The Christian Life Commission of the BGCT sponsors a leadership program for Senior Adults in Texas Baptist churches, including a semi-annual newsletter, *Senior Connections*, which includes thematic articles, a calendar of events, book reviews, with articles in Spanish and English. The Christian Life Commission is offering a model program, an online course for senior adult leaders, which will soon be available to churches throughout the state. This faith-based initiative is an excellent way to use information technology to provide resources for caring for older adults.

The diverse Baptist perspectives on matters of public funding and partnering are a major contribution to the national dialogue on charitable choice and faith-based initiatives, but the actual initiative Baptists are taking in providing faith-based services is an even greater contribution. Texas Baptist programs for older adults address issues from promoting independence to late stages of residential nursing care, from providing meals to computer-based leadership training. All of these activities can be clearly identified as based on the faith of the people planning and delivering these valued services.

NOTE

1. Charitable Choice provisions were included in section 104 of Welfare Reform legislation (the Personal Responsibility and Work Opportunity Reconciliation Act of 1996) with funding opportunities available to Welfare-to-Work and TANF programs. Charitable Choice was expanded in the Health and Human Services Reauthorization Act (1998) with money applied to community services and block grants, in the Children's Health Act (2000) applied to drug treatment programs of the Substance Abuse and Mental Health Services Administration, and the Community Renewal Tax Relief Act (2000) applied to drug abuse treatment and prevention programs. The Bush initiative, House Resolution 7 that moved to the Senate in the 107th Congress, also known as the Watts-Hall Community Solutions Act, sought to expand Charitable Choice and broaden the scope and extent of government financial collaboration with religious providers.

REFERENCES

Anderson, F. (1995). *Baptist Distinctives.* Richmond, VA: The Virginia Baptist Historical Society.

Baptist General Convention of Texas. (BGCT). (2001). Human Care Ministries Institutions. Retrieved August 25, 2001 from http://www.bgct.org/hwcb/default.htm

Baptist Joint Committee on Public Affairs & The Interfaith Alliance Foundation. (2001). *Keeping the faith: The promise of cooperation, the perils of government funding: A guide for houses of worship.* Washington, D.C.

Buckner Baptist Benevolences. (2001). Annual Report. Retrieved August 8, 2001 from http://www.buckner.org/pages/annual_report/annualreport2000/financials.html

Buckner ElderCare. (2001a). Buckner ElderCare Services. Retrieved September 14, 2001 from http://www.buckner.org/pages/_eldercare.html

Buckner Elder Care. (200lb). Buckner Eldercare Services Information Sheet. Nacogdoches, TX.

Buckner Retirement Services. (2001). *We Care.* Brochure.

Davis, D. (2001, February 7). Newsmakers. *Report from the Capital 56,* 3, 3. Baptist Joint Committee.

Estep, Jr., W. R. (1989). Religious freedom. *The Baptist Heritage Pamphlet Series.* The Historical Commission of the Southern Baptist Convention. 1989.

Foster, F. (2001, March 26). Baptist memorials opens Alzheimer's unit. *Baptist Standard*, p. 3.

Gaddy, C. W. (2001, July 17). Press release from the Interfaith Alliance Foundation Inc.

Goodwin, E. C. (1997). *Baptists in the Balance: The Tension between Freedom and Responsibility.* Valley Forge, PA: Judson Press.

Haag, J. (2001, June 4). Questions shape home's response to charitable choice. *Baptist Standard.* Retrieved August 8, 2001 from http://www.baptiststandard. com/2001/6_4/pages/charitable.html

Hall, K. (2001, March 12). A 'real world' perspective on faith-based funding debate. *Baptist Standard*, p. 6.

Hastey, S. L. (1979). Baptists and religious liberty. *The Baptist Heritage Pamphlet Series.* Nashville, TN: The Historical Commission of the Southern Baptist Convention.

McBeth, H. L. (1987). *The Baptist Heritage: Four Centuries of Baptist Witness.* Nashville, TN: Broadman.

Rogers, M. (1999). The wrong way to do right: Charitable choice and churches. *Welfare Reform and Faith-Based Organizations*, Davis, D. & Hankins, B. (Eds). Waco, TX: J.M. Dawson Institute of Church-State Studies, Baylor University.

SBC leader warms to charitable choice. (2001, May 14). *The Baptist Standard.*

Shurden, W. B. (2001). Turning points in Baptist history. *The Baptist Style for a New Century: Documents for Faith and Witness.* Jointly published by the Baptist History and Heritage Society and the William H. Whitsitt Baptist Heritage Society.

South Texas Children's Home (STCH). (2001). STCH policies and requirements. Retrieved August 8, 2001 from http://www.stch.org/policy.htm

Strode, T. (2001a, January 30). Bush establishes faith-based office; ERLC's Land urges ground rules. *Baptist Press News.*

Strode, T. (2001b, April 27). Faith-based summit reassures ERLC's Land. *Baptist Press News.*

Torbet, R. G. (1963). *A History of the Baptists.* (3rd ed.). Valley Forge, PA: Judson Press.

Walker, J. B. (2001, February 7). Buyer's remorse likely for those who embrace 'charitable choice.' *Report from the Capital 56,3,* 3. Baptist Joint Committee.

Wherefore the Faith-Based Initiative: A Commentary and Analysis

Ronald H. Field, MS

SUMMARY. Charitable Choice legislation has traveled a rocky road since 2001, both when presented as legislation in the U. S. Congress, as well as in the court of public opinion. From the perspective of the large faith-based agencies, the original 1996 Charitable Choice legislation was an adequate foundation for their work. Since the announcement of the president's faith-based initiative, diverting issues having to do with hiring practices, church-state issues, tax cuts, and sufficient funds to do the job have taken prominence. *[Article copies available for a fee from The Haworth Document Delivery Service: 1-800-HAWORTH. E-mail address: <docdelivery@haworthpress.com> Website: <http://www.HaworthPress. com> © 2004 by The Haworth Press, Inc. All rights reserved.]*

KEYWORDS. Faith-Based Initiatives, Charitable Choice, Congress, community, aged

President Bush's Faith-Based Initiative has been met with controversy and concern by persons from both ends of the political spectrum when it

---

Ronald H. Field is Vice President for Public Policy, Volunteers of America, 1660 Duke Street, Alexandria, VA 22314-3427 (E-mail: rfield@voa.org).

[Haworth co-indexing entry note]: "Wherefore the Faith-Based Initiative: A Commentary and Analysis." Field, Ronald H. Co-published simultaneously in *Journal of Religious Gerontology* (The Haworth Pastoral Press, an imprint of The Haworth Press, Inc.) Vol. 16, No. 1/2, 2004, pp. 99-105; and: *Faith-Based Initiatives and Aging Services* (ed: F. Ellen Netting, and James W. Ellor) The Haworth Pastoral Press, an imprint of The Haworth Press, Inc., 2004, pp. 99-105. Single or multiple copies of this article are available for a fee from The Haworth Document Delivery Service [1-800-HAWORTH, 9:00 a.m. - 5:00 p.m. (EST). E-mail address: docdelivery@haworthpress.com].

was first introduced in the President's inaugural address. Originally announced by the president on January 29, 2001 as his Faith-Based and Community Initiative, the controversial debates have focused more on the "charitable choice" and the separation of church and state aspects of the proposal.

Borrowing in part from the Clinton administration's establishment of a faith-based office in the Department of Housing and Urban Development (HUD) headed by a Catholic priest, as well as the President's own office of Faith-Based initiatives developed while he was governor of Texas, the Bush administration announced the creation of a White House Office of Faith-Based and Community Initiatives and five faith-based centers in the departments of Labor, Education, Justice, Health and Human Services (HHS), and HUD, each directed by a presidential appointee. In announcing his initiative, President Bush acknowledged that, in the face of our wealth as a nation, there is still too much poverty and despair. That point is clear:

- As many as 40 percent of our senior citizens live almost exclusively on Social Security income, a source that was established as social insurance against destitution, not as a retirement fund;
- Over a half million children are in foster care, more than one-fifth of whom are awaiting adoption;
- Approximately 1.5 million children have a parent in prison;
- Nearly twenty percent of American families with children live in poverty, whether working or not;
- Hundreds of thousands of our citizens are homeless and live on the streets, with homeless families now accounting for nearly 40 percent of that population; and
- With a desperate shortage of affordable housing across the country, 5 million households with occupants of all ages living in worst-case housing conditions that take half or more of their meager income for shelter, often in less than desirable conditions.

Recognizing the validity of those well-known facts and perhaps the constitutional mandate to provide for the common defense and general welfare of the people, the president said that government has a "solemn responsibility" to help meet the needs of the poor and of poor neighborhoods. "The indispensable and transforming work of faith-based and other charitable service groups must be encouraged. Government cannot be replaced by charities, but it can and should welcome them as partners," he said in his announcement (The White House, 2001a).

Of course, charities, including those with faith origins, have been partnering with government for many decades. As far back as the 1830s, Alexis de Tocqueville noted the important contributions such groups make to our social life as a country. It was churches and charities the government looked to after the Civil War to care for the nation's widows and orphans. Today, according to the Aspen Institute's Great Collisions Report, *What Is the Role of Faith-Based Institutions Today?* (Aspen Institute, 2002) the annual value of faith-based social service efforts is more than $36 billion.

So, what is all the fuss and bother? According to the White House, it is an unlevel playing field of regulatory and bureaucratic discrimination that prevents smaller faith-based and community organizations from competing for local, state, or federal social services grants. To prove their case, the administration directed each of the five new faith-based departmental centers to conduct a department-wide audit of the barriers to participation and delivery of social services and compile their findings in a report, which was issued in late August 2001. Among their findings were that

- A funding gap exists between the government and the grassroots: smaller groups, faith-based and secular, receive very little federal support relative to the size and scope of the social services they provide;
- There exists a widespread bias against faith- and community-based organizations in federal social service programs;
- Although legislation requires some restrictions on the full participation of faith-based organizations, many of the regulations are needlessly burdensome;
- Charitable Choice legislation passed by Congress has generally been ignored by federal, state, and local government administrators; and
- Despite such obstacles, some faith-based and community-based service groups have received government grants and contracts to deliver social services (The White House, 2001b. p. 2).

Indeed, despite many obstacles, a large number of locally focused, national faith-based organizations, such as Catholic Charities, Lutheran Services in America, United Jewish Communities, The Salvation Army, Volunteers of America, and others, have provided a large part of the nation's needed social services for a century or more, with government assistance that necessarily went beyond what could be raised privately through charitable giving. Without that government partnership, no amount of charity would have sufficed to meet the need. It still does not.

Unfortunately, the White House report took to task the very providers of social services it has been partnering with for those essential services as being "typically large and entrenched, in an almost monopolistic fashion" (The White House, 2001b, p. 2). despite the fact that they all operate in multiple fashion through locally organized nonprofit entities and parish structures in community after community across the country. Hardly monopolies and certainly community focused, they serve anybody that needs whatever service it is they provide without discrimination, as is their mission. Do all faith-based and community organizations that provide services and could use it get governmental funding? Probably not. Would they all qualify, despite their good works and intentions? Hard to say. Given all they perceive they would have to do to qualify, even with a lessening of regulatory burden, would they all still want government funds with which to operate? Again, probably not.

It is not so much a question of whether more local nonprofit organizations of whatever kind should get government money. Clearly, if there was sufficient money to disburse to a broader array of organizations that would deliver social services in an effective and efficient manner, they should be considered in the funding decisions. After all, faith-based services were eligible under the provisions of previously passed federal Charitable Choice laws as part of welfare reform in 1996, in Welfare-to-Work legislation in 1997, in the reauthorized Community Services Block Grant in 1998, and in SAMHSA's substance abuse prevention and treatment programs in 2000.

Unfortunately, as a first issue, there is widespread belief that federal and state funding appropriated to meet social service needs is too insufficient already to risk dilution for the sake of funding numerous new providers. In addition, there is general agreement on other important issues bearing on client protections that must be taken into consideration, among which are

- The capacity and competency of a local organization to administer a program and deliver the services;
- The ability to live up to accepted program and credentialing standards; and
- The necessity of being audited for fiscal and program accountability.

These were the major issues that swirled around the consideration of federal legislation in 2001. While the Bush administration had promised its own bill, it was left to Representatives J. C. Watts (R-OK) and Tony Hall (D-OH) to introduce H.R. 7, the Community Solutions Act. This bill would have created modest new tax incentives for charitable giving and expanded Charitable Choice to include an array of new programs, such as juvenile delinquency prevention, crime prevention, programs for seniors under the Older Americans Act, housing, job training, childcare, community development, domestic violence prevention and intervention, and hunger relief.

In addition, H.R. 7 clarified the conditions of Charitable Choice that would have allowed faith-based organizations to maintain their religious character and that of their facilities, and their right under Title VII of the Civil Rights Act of 1964 to staff on a religious basis, while not discriminating in any way against those they would serve. The bill was clear on the necessity to provide a secular alternative for clients who would object to a faith-based service and on the requirement that nobody could be made to participate in religious functions against their will.

Nevertheless, the bill was lacking in clarity on the key issues mentioned above, and became a test of the civil rights laws in hiring practices and the need to provide more adequate resources to make any of this happen. All of this was further burdened by a last minute amendment that would have given cabinet secretaries the authority to convert current grant programs into voucher programs, thus skirting federal and state hiring laws and potentially making the operations of and planning for significant social service programs much more difficult for providers. While H.R. 7 passed by a fairly close vote of 233-198 in the House of Representatives, it was not received well in the Senate.

Because of their sponsorship of an already existing bill aimed at expanding the tax incentives for charitable giving, Senators Rick Santorum (R-PA) and Joseph Lieberman (D-CT) were the lead members to fashion a bill to accomplish what the president wanted without getting into the same bind that H.R. 7 did. Working closely with the White House, their staffs and that of Senator Tom Daschle's Democratic leadership team drafted a bill that became generally acceptable to the faith community and its major service providers. In three sections, it would have expanded charitable giving tax incentives; provided for a Compassion Capital Fund to provide technical assistance to new and small faith and community organizations wanting to qualify for government grants and contracts to provide social services; and provided new resources for programs to serve children of incarcerated adults and teen mothers, as well as restore $1 billion in funding for the struggling Social Services Block Grant. All in all, it was a reasonable and welcomed piece of legislation that failed to see final action in the waning days of the first session of the 107th Congress because of disagreements between the Senate and the White House on provisions for an economic stimulus bill and the push to finish work on appropriations for fiscal year 2002, which began on October 1, 2001.

Instead, introduction of the bill was held up until February of 2002 when it became the Charity Aid, Recovery, and Empowerment (CARE) Act of 2002. Getting to that point was not easy, though, since many conservatives felt it did not go far enough to expand charitable choice and vowed to bring up a bill that did. Liberals, especially the civil rights community, felt it was too much of a church-state intrusion. They also felt that the tax incentives were too expensive, given the tax cuts passed earlier that year, which could very well create the rationalization of having to cut domestic discretionary spending on social services because of new budget deficits. Nevertheless, support by the president was enough to encourage senators Lieberman and Santorum to bring the bill forward. Unfortunately, it did not pass.

This is an ongoing debate. The CARE Act was reintroduced in the 108th Congress in 2003, but is still awaiting action by the Senate in 2004 over many of the same issues. What is clear is that the concepts it fosters are and will continue to be a philosophically contentious debate that attempts to further define the partnership roles of government and a broadened nonprofit social service community that might include more of a faith-based presence. The basic questions still persist, however: Will new, smaller, localized entities, whatever their affiliation, have the capacity and competency to successfully mount and deliver social services within accepted standards, and will there be enough money to maintain current services while attempting to fund a new group of service providers, or will we just be spreading our resources ever thinner?

These are important issues that hopefully will take into account the needs of the people seeking services, not just the political needs of policy makers. We will know the answers from the 108th Congress, which concludes its work this year. Clearly the current focus of this administration as well as the general public is overseas. However, it is important for all concerned to remain alert to the needs of the nation and of the nation's needy.

REFERENCES

Aspen Institute (2002). *What Is the Role of Faith-Based Institutions Today?* Aspen: Aspen Institute.

The White House (January 29, 2001a). Rallying the Armies of Compassion. Presidential statement, The White House. Washington, DC.

The White House (August, 2001b). Unlevel Playing Field: Barriers to Participation by Faith-Based and Community Organizations in Federal Social Service Programs. The White House. Washington, DC.

Managing Older Volunteers:
Implications for Faith-Based Organizations

Nancy L. Macduff

SUMMARY. Senior volunteers are often recruited from local congregations by religious affiliates and secular agencies in the community. Likewise they frequently carry out multiple roles in local congregations. Yet, congregations and their leaders–clergy and laity–do not always view their members as part of volunteer programs. In this article, the types of positions for which volunteers seem suited, the motivations of people who volunteer, and the accountability to a variety of stakeholders are considered in light of the professionalization of volunteer management. A case example illustrates the "quiet caring" that occurs when senior volunteers perform their roles from a congregational base, and the implications of changes in these roles as faith-based and community initiatives emerge. *[Article copies available for a fee from The Haworth Document Delivery Service: 1-800-HAWORTH. E-mail address: <docdelivery@haworth press.com> Website: <http://www.HaworthPress.com> © 2004 by The Haworth Press, Inc. All rights reserved.]*

KEYWORDS. Volunteerism, volunteer management, congregations, motivation, accountability

---

Nancy L. Macduff is affiliated with Macduff-Bunt Associates, 925 "E" Street, Walla Walla, WA 99362-3235 (E-mail: mba@bmi.net).

[Haworth co-indexing entry note]: "Managing Older Volunteers: Implications for Faith-Based Organizations." Macduff, Nancy L. Co-published simultaneously in *Journal of Religious Gerontology* (The Haworth Pastoral Press, an imprint of The Haworth Press, Inc.) Vol. 16, No. 1/2, 2004, pp. 107-122; and: *Faith-Based Initiatives and Aging Services* (ed: F. Ellen Netting, and James W. Ellor) The Haworth Pastoral Press, an imprint of The Haworth Press, Inc., 2004, pp. 107-122. Single or multiple copies of this article are available for a fee from The Haworth Document Delivery Service [1-800-HAWORTH, 9:00 a.m. - 5:00 p.m. (EST). E-mail address: docdelivery@haworthpress.com].

http://www.haworthpress.com/web/JRG
© 2004 by The Haworth Press, Inc. All rights reserved.
Digital Object Identifier: 10.1300/J078v16n01_07

It comes as little surprise that faith-based social service programs use volunteers. For many years, volunteers have been recruited from religious congregations by religiously affiliated organizations and secular agencies in local communities as part of the aging network's strategy to mobilize resources. Within local congregations, volunteers are the mainstay of program development, as they give of their time and talents to assist their faith traditions in addressing human needs. Indeed, it is difficult to fully inventory the numerous ways in which volunteers of all ages are recruited to perform numerous tasks designed to assist older persons in their communities.

The experiences of older or senior volunteers has been the subject of study for several decades. Trends in volunteering (Chambre, 1993), the difficulties inherent in defining the concept of volunteering among older adults (Fischer, Mueller, & Cooper, 1991), types of volunteer experiences and their impact on the health of elder volunteers (Jirovec & Hyduk, 1998), recruiting and retaining older volunteers (Kaplan, 1993; Morrow-Howell & Mui, 1989), and the receptivity among elders to post-retirement volunteering (Caro & Bass, 1997) are subjects that appear in the gerontological literature.

The focus of this article is on older volunteers in one type of faith-based organization–the local congregation. Beginning by recognizing that congregations of any faith tradition are volunteer programs, an overview of what is known about volunteer management is presented, followed by a faith-based case example. Implications of faith-based policy initiatives on the use of older volunteers concludes this article.

FAITH-BASED ORGANIZATIONS AND VOLUNTEER PROGRAMS

Most members of religious congregations can be identified as volunteers. In fact, clergy, staff, and leadership volunteers are "volunteer managers." Theirs is an associational structure in which people come to the congregation as members, donate to both operational and mission causes, and assume administrative or supportive roles within their local congregations. Paid staff, if they are available, manage numerous volunteers who perform roles on a weekly, even daily, basis.

As political agendas have moved further into devolution, localizing social services in community-based programs has become an accelerating part of that process. Given the internal and external nature of volunteering by members of religious congregations, it is important to explore the fundamentals of operating a program with volunteers as the workforce. One might ask, how does religious volunteer management compare with secular volunteer management? And how does the use of volunteers to deliver services change the nature and identity of a congregation? These questions are particularly important when faith-based organizations are viewed as resources by external sources with the expectation that they have a "value-added" dimension that traditional providers do not have.

There is ample literature on the organization and management of volunteer programs in both nonprofit and government (public) agencies. However, the suggested strategies for using volunteers have rarely been studied in faith-based groups like churches, synagogues, mosques, and the like (Wilson, 1983). Certainly, earlier works have examined various models used by religious congregations to contribute to, and even to deliver, services to older persons (e.g., Kimble, McFadden, Ellor, & Seeber, 1995; Tobin, Ellor, & Anderson-Ray, 1986). For example, by 1983 the Robert Wood Johnson Foundation had funded twenty-five projects in seventeen states as Interfaith Volunteer Caregiver Programs (IVCPs), designed to link volunteers with older persons needing in-home services and assistance. In 1987, the National Federation of Interfaith Volunteer Caregivers was founded; and by 1992 well over 1,200 congregations were involved in almost two hundred IVCPs (Seeber, 1995, p. 265). However, it is only recently that the concept of volunteering through congregational auspices has been studied in depth. Literature is more limited on senior volunteers in faith-based groups, even though they make up the bulk of many religious congregations.

VOLUNTEER MANAGEMENT AND THE OLDER VOLUNTEER

Practitioner literature is rich with information on how to organize and manage a successful professionally run volunteer program (Connors, 2001; Ellis, 1994; Macduff, 1996; Ellis, McCurley, 1998; Vineyard, 1999). Recommendations include such things as: targeted recruiting, screening through applications, developing position descriptions, and conducting interviews. There are managerial and recognition strategies that work especially well with volunteers. Also, there are methods of being accountable to funders, clients, boards, and to volunteers themselves.

Professionally managed volunteer programs are organized in ways similar to that of a corporate human resource department, with policies, applications, interviews, rewards (albeit small), newsletters, parties, and even an exit interview. The professional management of volunteers in secular organizations, and some faith-based groups, has evolved over time. Volunteer management has become more professional in the past 25 years. Today the Association for Volunteer Administration (the professional association for volunteer managers), has a 2,000-plus membership, a code of ethics, an international annual conference, and publishes *The Journal of Volunteer Administration*.

The move to "professionalize" the management of volunteers has been primarily driven by the research of academicians and practitioners, and by legal trends. The increasing study by academics and practitioners of volunteering has produced literature delineating what does and does not work. In 1975 there were two academic journals devoted to publishing research studies on nonprofit organizations and voluntary action: *The Journal of Volunteer Administration* and *The Nonprofit and Voluntary Sector Quarterly*, a publication of the Association for Research on Nonprofit Organizations and Voluntary Action (ARNOVA). Today there are numerous journals, including one that is Web-based.

Legal trends have also influenced the maturation of volunteer management as a field of practice. There has been an increase in lawsuits against charitable organizations and their volunteers. In addition, the "professionalizing" of volunteer programs has been driven by efforts to protect vulnerable populations, like seniors. Organizations want to avoid placing a volunteer in a position where she or he might be injured–such as a senior doing more lifting than is recommended for someone age 75. In some cases, concern for the welfare of the client and the volunteer has led administrators in nonprofit organizations to hire full-time volunteer managers. These administrators have also established programs to organize and supervise their unpaid work force. In other cases, the fear of lawsuits has forced administrators to take preventive steps to forestall legal action.

Today the average volunteer, senior or other, is likely to encounter paperwork, criminal record background checks, and interviews before being cleared to volunteer. The prospective volunteer encounters layers of accountability previously limited to work for pay. This call for greater accountability is widespread and covers all aspects of an organization's structure from the board through staff and to volunteers (Clohesy, 2000).

Given these trends, volunteer managers in the secular world utilize a wide variety of managerial strategies in order to ensure the healthy growth and operation of their volunteer workforce. Three areas are of paramount importance to them: (1) the types of positions for which volunteers seem suited (tasks or jobs available); (2) the motivations of people who volunteer; and (3) accountability to a variety of stakeholders. Each of these factors will be considered in light of what is known about volunteer management on one hand and faith-based organizations on the other.

Recognizing Types of Volunteer Positions

Schneider (1999) contends that social welfare (or care in the congregational environment) emanates from the community wishing to put its faith into action. This action, or translating faith into volunteer activities, follows religious, rather than secular norms, since a congregation's authoritative moral code is based on God's prompting. Thus, the moral code of the religious organization provides the guidelines that delineate the way in which its volunteers provide social services (Harris, 1994; Schneider, 1999). Depending on the congregation's belief system, these volunteer activities quite frequently extend beyond the needs of its members and into the surrounding community. For example, in the 1980s (in the wake of devolution, as the government reduced social service funding), mainline U.S. congregations were quietly delivering social services. These congregations provided money, volunteers, and facilities (Wineberg, 2001). Members provided direct services. They also served on the boards of local social service organizations (Harris, 1994).

Determining the type of social service project (and the types of tasks for volunteers) is a process often driven by religious practice and belief. The Quakers, for example, use a community process to determine not only the project, but also who will lead it. Unlike other denominations, where an individual can raise their hand and end up leading a big project, Quakers turn to their faith practices to determine if it is the right thing to do, and to determine if the person putting the idea forward is the right person to implement it. "Leadings" (someone suggests tackling a community project) are determined by a clearing process. "Clearing" involves several Friends meeting with the person who feels called to a Leading. Through the clearing process, the group discerns whether the Leading is a "true calling of the Spirit" or is only the will of the person who is bringing the idea forward (Schneider, 1999). Once a leading is declared a "ministry in the light," the entire congregation (Meeting) decides if it is united with that concern. If the project is accepted, the congregation puts the full force of its financial and social capital behind the endeavor. It is the equivalent of a seal of approval. Having this approval makes recruiting volunteers much easier.

Looking across a variety of denominational lines, Tobin et al. (1986) identified four basic service types engaged in by churches and synagogues who serve elders. These were: (1) providing religious programs, (2) serving as a host, (3) providing pastoral care programs, and (4) providing social services. Harris goes on to suggest that volunteer positions related to social service projects fall into six types:

1. Welfare projects of a social service nature that are ongoing–such as soup kitchens;
2. Indirect work that either helps the congregation, or provides funding for outside projects;
3. Informal care, which can be practical or emotional support for members of the congregation or those known to the congregation, i.e., shopping, cooking;
4. Informal care in a formal framework, such as a congregational group visiting a prison (however, they do what they wish when they get there);
5. Mutual aid, where the people who give the service are also the recipients of the service; and
6. Social integration, which brings those with needs into the congregation until they become full-fledged members of the faith-based group (Harris, 1998).

Given this list of projects, in a secular organization a staff member, volunteer coordinator, or client might suggest a job for volunteers. A position description would then be written, and recruiting would begin. However, in many faith communities, time is taken to see where God (or the Spirit) is leading them–individually and collectively. In other words, there is an ecclesiastical mandate that must be considered in determining what needs are addressed before even deciding who will be asked to volunteer.

What does it mean for the senior members of the congregation when a congregation determines that they will tackle a social service problem? Again, there is limited information on exactly how older persons in congregations are recruited to volunteer. However, considering what positions are assumed by older volunteers once they are recruited, a

Michigan study reviewed the types of roles held by senior volunteers and their younger counterparts. Black and Jirovic (1999) found that older congregational volunteers were focused primarily on clerical and fundraising tasks. Older women were often recruited to prepare or clean up for social events. The vast majority of older adults were segregated into activities involving other seniors. Low-income older adults provided service by delivering meals, and helping with personal care. The researchers noted that a substantial number of senior volunteers discontinued their service after only one year. This high dropout rate was an indication that non-challenging volunteer jobs are not any more appealing to seniors than to the general population.

If older volunteers are being recruited by faith communities, it is important to know what motivates and de-motivates volunteers. This leads to the second factor of paramount importance to volunteer managers–the motivations of people who volunteer.

Motivating Older Volunteers

Seniors are not solely influenced to volunteer by the tenets of their faith. They are also influenced by personal motivators and by the types of jobs available to them. It is helpful to know what research can tell us about these motivations.

In a study of 628 Baptist church volunteers in the Richmond, Virginia area, it was discovered that there were religious, personal, and altruistic reasons for volunteering. Adults over age 69 represented 18 percent of the sample (Black and Jirovic, 1999). In this study, there was a need to find challenging jobs, otherwise volunteers dropped out. Material rewards, such as meeting influential people, getting practical experience, learning a skill, and getting ahead in a career, were *negatively* correlated to volunteer commitment. People volunteered without the need for receiving exterior rewards. Respondents defined rewards in interior spiritual terms, such as being able to get beyond one's self, to feel more connected to God and with humankind. Respondents did not express a great need for outside affirmation in their work (Black and Jirovic, 1999).

Interestingly, none of the volunteers studied had job descriptions, contracts, or agreements for work. Having clear directions that will enable volunteers to do their best work is an essential tenet of the practitioner literature on managing the successful volunteer program. These Baptist volunteers received no training for their duties. Again, training is a primary part of preparing volunteers to successfully carry out their responsibilities in almost all secular volunteer programs. While job descriptions, contracts and training appear to add formality to the structure of care giving, it must be remembered that most congregations prefer (and are better at providing) the quiet and informal forms of caring.

In a different study, volunteers commented on the spiritual sustenance they received from participating in social service projects sponsored or operated by their faith community (Harris, 1998). Harris's research led her to conclude that volunteers are motivated by opportunities for self-fulfillment and autonomous work. These same volunteers did not expect to be managed, controlled, or monitored (Harris, 1995). For example, in one case, a volunteer leader who tried to give instructions to volunteers was criticized for being "too autocratic." The appeal of the work came from autonomous social services. There was little interest in the formality required by secular volunteerism. The study by Harris (1995) indicates that individual faith congregations have strong mores against any type of management or control over their volunteers.

While faith-based volunteers do not want to be managed, they do, indeed, face consequences when they do not meet the organization's role expectations or job performance. These consequences often negatively impact the activity and can create confusion between staff and volunteers. These negative consequences of unmet expectations can jeopardize volunteer loyalty. However, it is important to recognize that faith-based organizations and their volunteers bring a complex mix of motivations that do not always parallel secular volunteerism. This complex mixture of motivations occurs within the context of increasing accountability to multiple stakeholders, the third area of importance to volunteer managers.

Being Accountable to Multiple Stakeholders

Professionalism came gradually to the world of secular volunteerism. Many organizations were run by volunteers for decades. However, the programs offered by these organizations changed, enlisting more volunteers and taking on more social welfare programs, e.g., end poverty, increase literacy, address the scourge of HIV/AIDS. It became increasingly obvious that the more sophisticated and professional the management of modern volunteer programs, the more successful they became. The number of people recruited to do good works, and the hours donated continued to rise for those organizations using sophisticated volunteer management strategies.

"Professionalizing" volunteer initiatives means becoming more and more accountable. Organizations are accountable to volunteers by being clear about their expectations. When organizations utilize such things as position descriptions, applications, interviews, contracts, and the like, volunteers are willing to be accountable by providing personal information to the organization. Yet, these factors are the very items that research among older congregational volunteers indicates are not used or desired (Harris, 1995).

The call for accountability means that faith-based communities that want federal funding for their social service programs could be forced to put in place an infrastructure to manage their volunteers. This means that governing bodies adopt policies and procedures dealing with recruitment, screening, supervision, management, recognition, funding, and the evaluation of their volunteer programs. Larger programs might have to hire more staff to carry out the policies and procedures established by their governing bodies. And last, but by no means least, the individual volunteer will encounter additional job requirements, such as: completing an application, providing references, giving a job history, being fingerprinted for a criminal records background check, participating in training, having a yearly review of volunteer service, and attending the annual volunteer recognition banquet.

Volunteers from one religious-based organization were driven off by just such actions on the part of an eager executive director. Schneider (1999) reports that the involvement of volunteers from a particular religious community (who had founded the program) was threatened by an executive director who focused on professionalization and did not understand the role of volunteer service in this particular community of faith. One member called to volunteer and was told there were no slots available because the slots were being held for social work interns. His response was that the program, while using the name of the denomination, was no longer really a part of the faith-based body. If it were, there would have been room for him. By following secular norms, and not the cultural and religious practices of the faith-based group, "professionalization" can create barriers to volunteer involvement. In the case of this particular religious congregation, the establishment of social programs, the selection of a leader, the organization of the program, and the commitment of the congregation to volunteer is arrived at through a lengthy process of religious discernment. Volunteer labor comes to the project by its having a reputation within the religious community as an approved means to contribute to the social good. It is the ultimate recruiting technique (Schneider, 1999).

Filling out applications, meeting recruiting criteria, and other requirements of the secular world can run counter to the way senior volunteers end up working in a social service program organized through their faith community. Harris (1994) says that congregations often engage in social service using the "quiet care" model that is quite informal. When the task is challenging, congregations can also experience difficulty recruiting and keeping volunteers. One program for homeless people had volunteers cleaning up blood after a nasty fisticuffs broke out in a food line. Here was a situation of untrained and unsupported volunteers facing complex social problems (Harris, 1994).

This is not to say that faith-based organizations never apply the principles of volunteer management and accountability. In one congregation, volunteers were screened and selected, and then passed on to another volunteer for training before beginning their assignment. Another group set up lists of willing members and rotated their work during the year. They had great success at recruiting and keeping people using this method (Harris, 1995). It must be noted, however, that the most successful secular volunteer programs are ones with a full-time, paid volunteer manager who supervises the volunteers. Most religious congregations have a strong prohibition against controlling volunteers. As was noted earlier, one motivation for religious volunteers is autonomy. The studies reviewed for this paper repeatedly illustrate that control, manipulation, and "being sucked-in" jeopardize the loyal and continued work of the volunteer (Harris, 1995).

An anomaly is that in Harris's studies, she found volunteers who wanted constant support and approval from clergy, while others were quite vocal in saying that they did not think someone should be their "boss." In keeping with this, some volunteers became angry when they felt there was insufficient recognition of their work (Harris, 1995). A key rule in managing volunteers in the secular world is, "You can never say thank you too much." This axiom gives credence to the notion that the elements of managing volunteers in the secular world are much the same as those needed in the religious. In fact, Harris outlines the steps in the process that congregations can take to engage their volunteers:

- Determine what the volunteers of the congregation have to contribute (need)
- Motivate the members to volunteer and meet the need
  Match the people in the congregation to the various tasks required to attend to the need
- Provide support and guidance for the volunteers while they work to meet the need

- Recognize their contributions
- Provide continuity of leadership
- Work to promote positive volunteer and staff relations (Harris, 1995)

Given the importance of determining the types of positions that volunteers will assume, understanding the motivations of the persons who volunteer, and recognizing the increasing accountability to multiple stakeholders, there is much to think about in managing any volunteers. When it comes to volunteers in the context of a faith-based organization, the situation is even more complex. We now turn to a brief case example for illustrative purposes.

FRED: A CASE EXAMPLE

Fred walks slowly down the driveway to his car and drives to St. David's hospital kitchen to pick up ten meals to deliver to his special friends–seniors struggling to live independently. At age 77, Fred lives with his wife of 55 years, goes to Rotary Club meetings, and does lots of volunteer work. Several years ago, the minister at his church, St. Margaret's, announced at a Sunday service that the church was providing drivers for a meal-delivery program for seniors. Anyone interested should see her. Fred chatted with Reverend Barbara. She called the folks at St. David's. Two days later, he was delivering his first meals as a Meals Program driver. He loves his delivery job and the people he visits. He knows he is really helping; and he likes being busy. He also often helps out by driving the seniors to medical appointments, as well. Recently, one man even asked Fred for help with his taxes.

Meal delivery is only the beginning of Fred's active volunteer service. He also visits daily with a professional colleague felled by a massive stroke. He helps his colleague get into the car and then drives him around the countryside. For years, he took this man to a water aerobics class at the local swim center.

At St. Margaret's, Fred is the chairperson of a committee that works with three community food banks. The church committee works to raise money for perishable food. They also goad the congregation into donating non-perishable items on a regular basis. Fred is known to humorously bar the doors to the nave if a church member arrives without a can of foodstuff before Sunday services.

Fred in Context

Fred is one of the 34 percent of Americans over age 75 who do regular volunteer work. As a meals-delivery driver, he volunteers through a faith-based organization. Through his church, he gives service to a hospital-based volunteer program. As a volunteer, he isn't alone. Of individuals age 55-64, 48 percent do volunteer work. Of individuals age 65-74, 45 percent volunteer. The number of seniors reporting doing volunteer work has increased since 1988. In 1988, 40 percent of those age 65-74 report volunteering regularly. Among those over age 75, only 29 percent said that they did volunteer work (Independent Sector, 1996, p. 54). It is likely that the increasing health and active life style of seniors is contributing to this rise in the numbers of seniors who volunteer.

It is also a fact that those who regularly attend church, synagogue, or mosque services are more likely to volunteer than those who do not. Half of those attending religious services volunteer; while among those who do not attend regular religious services, only one-third volunteer (Independent Sector, 1996, p. 90). In a North Carolina survey of 128 congregations, 87 percent of them provide volunteers, or other in-kind services, to social welfare programs in their community (Wineberg, 2001, p. 66). Most religious congregations are part of the social welfare fabric of their community. They often deliver that service through secular organizations. In some cases the relationship has evolved from providing volunteers and allowing the use of their facilities to a more complex and comprehensive relationship (Wineberg, 2001).

Volunteers like Fred engage in activities that link religious groups with agencies that deliver services to seniors. A typical mobile meals program may work out of a senior center, a kitchen in a local hospital or school, or even out of a church. These are not new activities; they have been going on for decades. Interestingly, because the 1996 Charitable Choice provisions were tied to welfare reform, the rhetoric of the faith-based initiative has focused on social services involving children (mentoring, tutoring, youth development, and anti-gang projects) and families (homelessness, drug addiction, abuse and neglect), with rarely a word about service by or for seniors (American Demographics, 2001, p. 22). It is likely, however, that some faith-based organizations, with a strong core of senior volunteers, will apply for projects to provide social service to seniors and others. Should public dollars be used to mobilize this cadre of volunteers in additional ways, it is possible that a more formalized, perhaps professionalized, volunteer management approach might be considered.

Therefore, one question for Fred's church to deal with is: How will the organization's "Army of Compassionate" volunteers be influenced by governmental funding? If proposed legislation is enacted, the details of how faith-based organizations go about delivering social services could be looked at in the light of increasing accountability trends. This scrutiny could impact Fred and the seniors he visits. Will the casual, non-institutional form of volunteering, so common in faith-based organizations, continue? Or will concerns for legal and financial liability force change–potentially driving seniors away from the jobs that they love? As with most policy implementation, the devil is in the details.

IMPLICATIONS

There is scant literature on senior volunteers and programs in faith-based communities. However, enough tantalizing information exists to warrant some observations, pleas for further study, and recommendations about how a faith-based volunteer program might begin to examine its use of older volunteers.

Volunteering by seniors in faith-based organizations is thriving. This phenomenon is nothing new. Several sources report increased volunteer activity over the past twenty years in the numbers and hours given by those over age 55. Volunteering in many faith-based organizations is done by those over age 55. This fact will impact the types of programs faith-based communities are willing to support with their time and money. Most senior volunteer efforts appear to be focused on the faith-based institutions' needs, and not as greatly on external social services.

The standards for operating a secular volunteer program can run counter to the world of volunteering by the faithful. The professional standards for volunteers might hamper "spiritually" driven ways of coming to the actual volunteer activity. There is little research on strategies to effectively manage volunteers in the religious setting. Successful programs do exist. They need to be studied in order to provide lay and clerical leaders with the information they need to run their own successful programs.

Accountability is the highest mountain for the faith-based social service program to climb. What mechanisms are in place to screen volunteers to protect those served? What policies are in place to protect the assets of the institution from inappropriate volunteer behavior? How are volunteers protected from inappropriate activities? Doing good in the 21st century is decidedly more complicated than in the past.

The scant literature available on the difference in volunteer motivations for older and younger volunteers could impact the success of the most sincere efforts to solve serious community problems. Senior volunteers appear to be as altruistic as their younger counterparts. They are also driven by wanting to keep busy and active. The appeal to bring in older volunteers must be different from that aimed at young singles.

Complicating motivation and accountability are the types of jobs available to older volunteers. One study reviewed indicated that faith-based volunteers want challenging jobs, but a look at actual volunteer positions held by senior volunteers reveals their jobs to be little more than clerical or housekeeping support for the programs. Creating programs to change communities or people is a complicated, hands-on business. If the hands-on positions are limited to the young or to the paid, seniors may opt to take their services where they can really make a difference. The issue of the types of tasks available for senior volunteers might well determine whether anyone from a congregation is willing to serve.

Schneider's (1999) study suggests that successful faith-based programs do three things in order to provide effective social service. First, they translate their faith into action. How is what the volunteers do connected to the mission and purpose of the organization? Can volunteers, clients, administrators make a direct link from who they are to what they do? Second, the problem is conceptualized by the faith-based group. They know how to solve this problem. It involves building alliances, working cooperatively with staff, clients, stakeholders. It involves knowing specifically what volunteers may or may not do. Solving the problem means matching the right people with the right jobs inherent in meeting the client's needs. The solution has a clear concept and picture of how volunteer efforts can impact the problem. Third, they develop effectiveness in working with specific populations. Once the program activities and the volunteers are in place, there are multiple ways to communicate with volunteers, clients, and administrators. There is feedback from clients to volunteers, from volunteers to staff, from staff to governing or oversight bodies, and vice versa. Evaluation and recognition are part of running an effective volunteer program.

In conclusion, policy-makers, clergy, volunteer managers, academics, and the media all debate the details of using religious institutions in implementing social welfare programs. Meanwhile, Fred quietly goes about his rounds of volunteering, without fanfare or tangible rewards–never having filled out a form, never having sat for an interview. As one of the millions of members of the "Army of Compassion," this foot soldier continues on with his "quiet caring."

REFERENCES

American Demographics, Paul, P., "Church and State: Divide or Unite?" (August, 2001), 22-23.

Black, B. & Jirovic, R.L. (1999). Age differences in volunteer participation. *The Journal of Volunteer Administration, XVII*(2), 38-47.

Caro, F.G., & Bass, S.A. (1997). Receptivity to volunteering in the immediate postretirement period. *The Journal of Applied Gerontology, 16*(4), 427-441.

Chambre, S.M. (1993). Volunteerism by elders: Past trends and future prospects. *The Gerontologist, 33*(2), 221-228.

Clohesy, W.W. (2000). Altruism and the endurance of the good. *Voluntas: International Journal of Voluntary and Nonprofit Organizations, 11*(3), 237-253.

Connors, T. (Ed.). (2001). *The nonprofit handbook* (3rd ed.). New York, NY: John Wiley & Sons, Inc.

Ellis, S. (1994). *The volunteer recruitment book*. Philadelphia, PA: ENERGIZE, Inc.

Fischer, L.R., Mueller, D.P., & Cooper, P.W. (1991). Older volunteers: A discussion of the Minnesota senior study. *The Gerontologist, 31*(2), 183-194.

Giving and Volunteering in the United States, 1996, Independent Sector, 1996, Washington, DC.

Harris, M. (1994). *Care by congregation, working paper 15*. London, England: Centre for Voluntary Organisation at the London School of Economics.

Harris, M. (1995). *The church is the people, working paper 16*. London, England, Centre for Voluntary Organisation at the London School of Economics.

Harris, M. (1998). *Organizing God's work*. New York, NY: St. Martin's Press.

Herman, R. (Ed.). (1994). *The Jossey-Bass handbook of nonprofit leadership and management*. San Francisco, CA: Jossey-Bass.

Independent Sector, Jalanodoni, N., Hume, K. (2001), "America's Family Volunteers: Civic Participation is a Family Matter." Washington, DC.

Jirovec, R.L., & Hyduk, C.A. (1998). Type of volunteer experience and health among older adult volunteers. *Journal of Gerontological Social Work, 30*(3/4), 29-42.

Kaplan, M. (1993). Recruiting senior adult volunteers for intergenerational programs: Working to create a "jump on the bandwagon" effect. *The Journal of Applied Gerontology, 12*(1), 71-82.

Kimble, M.A., McFadden, S. H., Ellor, J.W., & Seeber, J.J. (Eds.) (1995). *Aging, spirituality, and religion: A handbook*. Minneapolis, MN: Fortress Press.

Macduff, N. (1985). *Volunteer recruiting and retention*. Walla Walla, WA: MBA Publishing.

McCurley, S. (1998). *Essential volunteer management* (2nd ed.). London, England: Directory of Social Change.

Morrow-Howell, N. & Mui, A. (1989). Elderly volunteers: Reasons for initiating and terminating service. *Journal of Gerontological Social Work, 13*(3/4), 21-34.

Schneider, J. (1999). Trusting that of God in everyone. *Nonprofit and Voluntary Sector Quarterly, 28*(3), 269-295.

Seeber, J.J. (1995). Congregational models. In Kimble, M.A., McFadden, S. H., Ellor, J.W., & Seeber, J.J. (Eds.). (1995). *Aging, spirituality, and religion: A handbook*, pp. 253-269. Minneapolis, MN: Fortress Press.

Tobin, S.S., Ellor, J.W., & Anderson-Ray, S.M. (1986). *Enabling the elderly: Religious institutions within the community service system.* Albany, NY: State University of New York Press.

Vineyard, S. (1999). *Marketing for volunteer managers.* Washington, D.C.: The Points of Light Foundation.

Wilson, M. (1983). *How to mobilize church volunteers.* Minneapolis, MN: Augsburg Press.

Wineberg, B. (2001). *A limited partnership.* New York, NY: Columbia University Press.

Faith Organizations
and Ethnically Diverse Elders:
A Community Action Model

Terry Tirrito, PhD
Gil Choi, PhD

SUMMARY. In this article we argue that faith organizations should become involved in developing social service programs for older adults in the community. In the current political climate, the government is providing fewer social service programs, and future prospects for services are bleak. The literature provides evidence that religion and faith-based organizations are important in the lives of Americans, particularly the current cohort of ethnically diverse elders. Our earlier Korean church study found that Korean older people benefit from church-based services and church-involved, older Koreans had higher rates of well-being. Churches remain untapped resources and we believe they should be extensively involved in provision of community programs. We offer a twelve-step model for the development of community programs under the auspices of faith organizations: The Faith-Based Community Action Model (FBCAM). *[Article copies available for a fee from The Haworth Document Delivery Service: 1-800-HAWORTH. E-mail address: <docdelivery@haworthpress.com> Website: <http://www.HaworthPress.com> © 2004 by The Haworth Press, Inc. All rights reserved.]*

Terry Tirrito and Gil Choi are affiliated with the College of Social Work, University of South Carolina, Columbia, South Carolina.

[Haworth co-indexing entry note]: "Faith Organizations and Ethnically Diverse Elders: A Community Action Model." Tirrito, Terry, and Gil Choi. Co-published simultaneously in *Journal of Religious Gerontology* (The Haworth Pastoral Press, an imprint of The Haworth Press, Inc.) Vol. 16, No. 1/2, 2004, pp. 123-142; and: *Faith-Based Initiatives and Aging Services* (ed: F. Ellen Netting, and James W. Ellor) The Haworth Pastoral Press, an imprint of The Haworth Press, Inc., 2004, pp. 123-142. Single or multiple copies of this article are available for a fee from The Haworth Document Delivery Service [1-800-HAWORTH, 9:00 a.m. - 5:00 p.m. (EST). E-mail address: docdelivery@haworthpress.com].

Digital Object Identifier: 10.1300/J078v16n01_08

KEYWORDS. Faith organizations, older adults, community action programs

HISTORICAL MISSION OF FAITH ORGANIZATIONS

Historically, religion was intertwined with community and social institutions. The church was often the sole provider of services for the poor, the elderly, the orphaned, and the needy. In modern times, the original mission of the church as an institution of community service has changed, with faith organizations focusing primarily on the individual's spiritual life. Religious organizations served community functions, such as helping the poor with shelter; housing and caring for the sick, the old, and the disabled; and providing food to families in need. Charity and almsgiving can be traced to references in the Bible.

Until the Middle Ages, churches provided social services to local communities. After the Protestant Reformation the separation of church and state changed the church's mission and limited its role in civic life. In Colonial America, the separation of church and state became the central focus of the Puritans who urged government to take on more responsibility for solutions to societal problems. Charitable deeds remained the focus of communities and churches until the early 20th century when government assumed more responsibility for social problems.

During the Roosevelt administration, the creation of government-sponsored social services became a national priority as evidenced by the passage of the Social Security Act of 1935. The Kennedy and Johnson years continued the federal government's expansion into social service provision with the passage of both the Medicare and Medicaid Acts in 1965, ushering in the Great Society era.

THE ERA OF SCARCE PUBLIC RESOURCES

The Reagan-Bush administrations introduced a new era of diminishing federal responsibility through devolution. The policy of devolution of social services to the local level contributed to more federal budget cuts for social programs (Cnaan, 1999; Wineburg, 2001).

President Reagan paved the way for the most dramatic reversal in social welfare policy since the 1930s. Wineburg (2001) states, "if local citizens, clergy, agency planners, or scholars choose to look closely at the evolution of human services in communities across the United States, they would find that the path has been laid for bringing religious, government, and private non-profit agencies to the planning table" (p. 32).

The devolution trend in national government spending limits programs for social services to persons of all ages and challenges the ability of local governments to meet the ever increasing needs of communities (Sherman & Viggiani, 1996). Social service programs traditionally provided by community social agencies such as family counseling, mental health counseling, crisis counseling, support groups, respite services, educational programs, caregiver training, and a variety of health and nutritional programs are increasingly competing for resources. If devolution proceeds as expected, scarce, uncertain resources may mean that community agencies will look more and more to faith organizations as providers.

The end of welfare as it was known in the 1990s found community members with cuts in food stamp programs, Supplemental Social Insurance, Medicaid, and child welfare programs. Communities with dwindling financial resources are being challenged to meet the needs of their citizens. As policy-makers concede that the federal government cannot meet all needs, President George W. Bush is supporting the efforts of faith-based and community initiatives to provide for the unmet and under met needs of communities.

FAITH ORGANIZATIONS HAVE RESOURCES

The church has a long history in the provision of tangible support and aid in times of crisis (Taylor, 1993; Tobin, Ellor & Anderson-Ray, 1986). In the early 20th century the church-based social agency represented the "active social consciousness of the church in society" (Netting, 1984, p. 417). Churches are described as ontological communities that symbolize communities of meaning and ontological communities often become the heart of a community (Bruggemann, 2002). Ontological religious communities are cultural, social, and ethnic centers for members of particular groups such as Muslims, Jews, Asians, or African-Americans.

Religious institutions form the largest network of voluntary associations in American society. Statistical data report about 500,000 local churches, synagogues, temples and mosques in America (Bruggemann, 2002, p. 302). Ontological communities can often supplement the perceived and tangible missing components of modern life. When primary social systems fail, ontological communities can fill the void. In some cities of the Northeast, the majority of social services are provided by religious organizations (Bruggemann, 2000). Nationally, there is a growing recognition that faith organizations are untapped resources for social services for older adults (Lewis, 1994).

Billingsley (1999) surveyed nearly a thousand black churches across the country to examine social service activities provided by African-American churches. He found a variety of programs including some for family support, parenting, substance abuse, youth-at-risk, role modeling, job training, and financial assistance. The Brookland Baptist Church in Columbia, South Carolina, provides a credit union for members to start small businesses (personal communication, 2001). Faith organizations support and staff day care programs, respite care programs, and shelters. The Protestant and Catholic churches, Buddhist temples and Muslim mosques, following their traditional roles, often provide social services to meet the needs of congregations and neighboring communities. The faith community's assets are invaluable resources for community programs.

The resources of the church include congregations of volunteers and facilities with space for community activities. Some churches currently provide space for Alcoholics Anonymous meetings and other support group meetings (Cnaan, 1999). Churches are used for assessment centers or to provide help with dementia related problems such as respite programs, support groups, counseling centers, and referral programs. Churches offer services for older persons who live alone and have little or no family contact. Volunteer groups for the sick aged and mutual help groups can be linkages to community agencies.

Faith organizations provide social services to their communities. Cnaan (1999) and Wineburg (2001) describe the intense involvement of faith organizations in the distribution of social services in the communities of Greensboro, North Carolina, and Philadelphia, Pennsylvania. Wineburg's Greensboro study examined community social service delivery in a small Southern city and reported that 84% of responding congregations offered at least one in-house service, such as counseling; 39% offered services to members of the community; 89% provided counseling services; 34% housed programs such as Alcoholics Anonymous, Narcotics Anonymous, Al-Anon, Alateen, and/or Overeaters Anonymous; 87% provided volunteers for shelters, and feeding programs; 44% worked with neighborhood groups, and 40% donated food to the food bank (p. 83).

Examples of faith-based social services include New York City's Partnership for the Homeless, started in 1982, by a handful of religious leaders. It addresses the needs of the overwhelming number of homeless persons in the city. The Oakhurst Baptist Church in Atlanta inspired over seventy other congregations to provide services for the homeless in Atlanta. Catholic orders of nuns and brothers provide church-based services for people with mental health problems including Alzheimer's disease, child welfare programs and health services. The First Baptist Church in Philadelphia provides Alcoholics Anonymous and Narcotics Anonymous programs for an average of five hundred persons a day (Cnaan, 1999). An innovative program is the Willow Creek Community Church Program in Illinois which offers an active car-repair service. Weekend repairmen repair the cars of fellow parishioners who cannot afford professional services. In 1993 this congregation gave away eighty-five automobiles to indigent single mothers. The Mendenhall Bible Church in Mississippi was established in the 1970s with only 125 members and an abandoned school building. With two hundred volunteers it remodeled the building which now maintains a business complex, a health clinic, law office, thrift shop, elementary school and recreation center (Cnaan, 1999, p. 194). In the United States, religious communities are involved in social service provision "to a degree unimagined and unacknowledged" (Cnaan, 1999, p. 157). Older adults need to be included more extensively in the populations who seek and receive social services through faith-based organizations.

THE IMPORTANCE OF RELIGION TO OLDER AMERICANS

In the United States there are 34,933,000 persons over 65 years of age and 4,368,000 over 85 years of age with 68,000 centenarians (U.S. Census, 2000). Improved medical care has contributed to longer life expectancy. Because of disability, chronic health problems, high rates of depression, anxiety, and substance abuse among aging baby boomers, there are predictions of near epidemic mental health problems among older persons in the first half of the 21st century (Koenig, 1995). Political issues regarding Medicare and Medicaid spending demonstrate that it is not clear how much and from what sources funding will be available for future geriatric health care. With demographic data indicating a continuous growth in older adults who also demonstrate a reluctance to use government-sponsored programs, it may well be the faith organizations that will assume the organization and distribution of social services to future cohorts of aging adults. The programs traditionally provided by community social agencies such as family counseling, mental health counseling, crisis counseling, support groups, respite services, educational programs, caregiver training, and a variety of health and nutritional programs may soon become the province of faith communities. Within this era of devolution, it is important to understand the roles played by faith-based and community initiatives in the lives of community members.

From primitive to modern times religion is strongly intrinsic in human life, thus the church, synagogue or mosque has a social responsibility to its congregation. As Simmons (1991) states, "if we don't who will?" (p. 17). Religion is important to Americans and in particular to older persons. Durkheim (1915) describes religion as "something eminently social" (p. 22) and describes faith organizations as having a function "to help us live." He claims that "nearly all the great social institutions have been born in religion" (p. 466). The evidence of the importance of religion to modern Americans is found in the data on American membership in religious bodies:

- Protestant (includes Latter-day Saints, and Jehovah's Witnesses) = 86,684,000
- Roman Catholic = 58,568,000
- Buddhist = 19,000,000
- Jews (includes Orthodox, Conservative, and Reform) = 5,981,000
- Old Catholic, Polish National Catholic, and American = 950,000
- Eastern = 3,976,000 (U.S. Census, 2000)

Over 76% of church and synagogue members are over 50 years of age (U.S. Census, 2000). A Gallup poll reported that 71 percent of Americans claim to be members of a church or synagogue and 41 percent report having attended church seven days prior to the survey (Cnaan, 1997, p. 220). Religious affiliation is positively correlated to life satisfaction in older adults (Tobin, 1985). According to Tobin, Ellor and Anderson-Ray (1986) three out of four persons 60 years and older report that religion is important in their lives; (2) four out of five persons older than 65 years attend church or synagogue regularly; and (3) evidence suggests that people maintain their religious beliefs throughout their lives and that the current cohort of older adults has been religious throughout their lives and continues to be so as they age (p. 64).

Religious affiliation is reported as an influential force that can positively enhance the well-being of older persons (Hungelmann, Kenkel-Rossi,

Klasser, & Stollenwerk, 1996). Church and synagogue attendance is lowest among those in their 30s, peaks in the late 50s and early 60s (60% of this age group attends religious services), and slowly declines in the 70s. Older adults, with over 60% attending religious services, exceed any other age group in this observance. People over age 65 years are the most likely to be affiliated with church groups or fraternal associations (Koenig, George, & Seigler, 1988, p. 305). The decline in attendance at formal services after age 70 may be attributed to health problems or lack of transportation to church functions.

Religiousness, whether described as institutional or personal, correlates positively with better morale, stronger coping skills, and better physical and mental health. For example, some studies found that depression and alcohol abuse are less prevalent in religious older adults (Zucker, Fair, & Branchey, 1987). Hypertension, anxiety, and cardiac problems are influenced by religious behaviors (Krause, 1991; Levin & Markides, 1985). Older persons who are religious are less depressed and have better mental health (Koenig, George, & Seigler, 1988). Older people who are religious are happier, have better coping mechanisms, less depression, and better physical and mental health (Johnson, 1995). Therefore, in light of the trust and religious/spiritual bonds that have been created, the church family "may be called on to serve as surrogate family for the treatment of a variety of ills which the family of birth is unable to handle" (Simmons, 1991, p. 24).

OLDER ADULTS PREFER CHURCH BASED SOCIAL SERVICES

The literature indicates that older persons prefer social services delivered by faith organizations rather than by community agencies. Gulledge (1992) describes clergy as the first persons contacted when families are in crisis. In another study, older persons were asked which programs they would be willing to attend at their places of worship. Over 55% responded that they sought programs relating to emotional health; 24% wanted financial programs; 42% said health programs; 31% said legal programs; 49% said programs relating to personal needs; 50% said recreation and educational programs. Over 70% of the respondents reported that they would be more willing to attend social service programs in their places of worship than at a community agency (Tirrito & Spencer-Amado, 2000, p. 59).

Tirrito and Euster (1994) surveyed older adults regarding types of social services provided by their churches. A small number (2%) reported having formal social service programs such as adult day care or group support programs. However, an interesting finding was that more than 40% of congregations did not provide any special programs for their older congregants (Tirrito & Euster, 1994, p. 4). Recognizing the importance of faith organizations is particularly relevant when one considers the importance of religion to older and ethnically diverse Americans.

ETHNIC CHURCHES AND OLDER AMERICANS

There is evidence that religion is important in the lives of people of ethnic cultures and some studies report that the church is an integral part of support networks for African Americans, Korean-Americans, and Hispanic Americans (Atchley, 1998). A study of over eighteen hundred Hispanic Americans reports that Hispanic Americans over age 55 were twice as likely to seek help from the church than from any other community agency (Koenig & Weaver, 1998).

Ethnic minority churches are a tradition in American life (Reid, Linder, Sheeley, & Stout, 1990). The ethnic church serves a predominantly homogeneous population. Reid et al. described ethnic churches as "one of the first major acts of a settled immigrant community" (p. 84). Ethnicity (from the Greek word ethos, which means "nation" or "peoplehood") is the socialization process by which individuals inherit a sense of identity and common culture from their national, religious, or racial group. Ethnic identity and religion are inextricably linked. In many immigrant groups ethnicity and religion are mutually reinforcing (Reid et al., 1990). In many large urban areas the Catholic Church serves an ethnic population (Petersen & Lee, 1975). Other ethnic churches are the Russian and Greek Orthodox Churches, which serve a particular ethnic group.

Protestant immigrant churches gradually became less ethnically homogenous and more integrated in the melting pot of Protestant America, but as the mother tongue gave way to English among second-generation Protestant immigrants, church membership in ethnic churches was of immense importance to preserving the culture of the ethnic group. Father Andrew Greeley (cited in Reid et al., 1990), a well-known Catholic sociologist, stated, "many people need a sense of peoplehood and desire to find it in an ethnically homogeneous inner life of church and family" (p. 570).

The importance of ethnic churches in the lives of African-Americans was apparent during the Civil Rights Movement. The African American Church remains involved in the health, transportation, and social services of its community (Logan, 1996). Data from the National Survey of Black Americans indicate a high degree of religious commitment among older black adults (Taylor, 1993). Older black adults have a higher probability of being religiously affiliated, of having attended religious services as an adult, and of being a church member than their white counterparts (Taylor, 1993). Today, social and political functions are a natural function of the African-American Church as a result of its role as an agency of social control during slavery (Smith, 1993). Other ethnic groups, such as Korean-American groups, have benefited from faith-based services.

THE KOREAN-AMERICAN CHURCH: AN EXAMPLE OF FAITH-BASED SERVICES

According to the 2000 U.S. Census, Koreans accounted for 11.6% of the Asian-American population. In 2000, the adult Korean population over 55 years of age numbered 79,788, or 10%, and those over 65 years of age numbered 35,247, or 4.4% (U.S. Census, 2000). Protestant Christianity is a major influence in the Korean-American community. Reid et al. (1990) claim "the establishment of a church was often among the first collective actions taken by Koreans after their arrival" (p. 85).

The Korean Church provides a base for ethnic identification. From 1910 to 1945 when the Japanese occupied Korea, churches provided places where the community could gather to support the Korean independence movement. The Korean Church later became a source of support for North Korean families under Communist rule. The Korean-American community has grown tremendously since 1975, and the Protestant Church has been a central institution in this community. It is estimated that there are about 1,000 Korean-American churches in the United States.

Korean churches play a significant role in Korean immigrants' adjustment to new environments in the United States. Choy (1979) reported that the Korean Church: (1) functions as a social center and as a source for cultural identification; and (2) serves an educational function by teaching American-born Koreans the Korean language, history, and culture. Kim (1979) reported that Korean churches function as brokers between their church members and bureaucratic institutions of the larger society. Hurh and Kim (1990) argued that "among the majority of

Korean immigrants, the religious need (meaning), the social need (belonging), and the psychological need (comfort) for attending the Korean church are inseparable" (p. 31). In a study of the Korean Protestant Church, Hurh and Kim (1990) analyzed the religious participation patterns of 622 Korean immigrants. They found that regardless of their length of residence, sex, age, level of education, economic status, or socio-cultural assimilation, respondents participated actively in church functions.

Choi and Tirrito (1999) researched the programs and activities offered to older adult members attending Korean churches. Data on demographic trends in each church, each pastor's level of knowledge of aging issues, and each pastor's gerontological training were collected. The availability of church-based programs and activities for older adults was measured in eleven different categories, including spiritual well-being, emotional and mental health, employment, referral, health care, personal needs, recreation and leisure, meaningful opportunities, continuing education, clubs, and visitations. Pastoral home visits were the most frequently reported service program provided by the churches (reported by 97% of participants).

Other types of programs frequently reported included visitation for the hospitalized (94.1%), pastoral counseling (88.2%), helping older adults become actively involved in church affairs (88.2%), group tours (82.4%), making doctors' appointments (79.4%), providing transportation (76.5%), and continuing education for affirming values and dignity of older persons (73.5%). Programs offered much less frequently include seminars on mental health (26.5%), English classes (26.5%), lectures on aging issues (17.6%), caregivers' training on stress management and care-burden (14.7%), and crafts (2.9%).

The findings of this study suggest that older Korean adults enjoy enhanced life satisfaction from participation in church activities. The researcher used the Cornell personal adjustment scale (Thompson, Streib, & Kosa, 1960) to measure satisfaction with life, dejection and hopelessness perceived by older adults. The greater the frequency of older Korean adults' attendance at Sunday services and church activities, the higher the ratings on happiness and life satisfaction. In addition, older respondents expressed feelings of increased life satisfaction when they engaged in such activities as Bible reading, prayer services, and listening to religious programs via radio, television, or tape. The practice of prayer and its provision of a sense of connection with God and with fellow church members may serve as a source of comfort, peace, strength, harmony, and support. Thus, the combination of these factors seems to contribute to feelings of well-being. Service providers should be aware of the role Korean churches play in addressing the spiritual needs as well as the emotional and mental health, economic, recreational, health, employment, continuing education, and legal needs of Korean older adults. As the study indicates, the psychological well-being of elderly Koreans is strongly and positively associated to programs, activities, and social support provided by the church.

One of the major problems for Korean American older persons is the underutilization of community social services. The Choi and Tirrito (1999) study revealed that only 13% of the respondents had visited social service agencies or used social services in spite of met mental and social service needs. Racial and cultural bias in service delivery may deter elderly Koreans from seeking service. Their help-seeking behaviors and self-disclosure patterns may be different from others' in the dominant culture. Language barriers certainly impede them from learning about services and interacting with service providers. Shortages of bilingual and culturally sensitive service providers may prevent them from seeking help. A striking feature of this study is its discovery that Korean churches may function as the major agents for provision of mental and social services that formal service agencies have failed to provide older adults.

LINKING DIVERSE ELDERS AND FAITH ORGANIZATIONS: A MODEL

In examining the rationale for the church as a service provider, the literature points to the failure of community social service agencies to provide needed services to older adults. Netting, Thibault and Ellor (1988) found evidence that older adults, particularly ethnic older persons, underutilized community social services. Older adults infrequently use community mental health services and consequently, older adults are frequently untreated for depression, dementia and alcohol and drug abuse. Koenig predicts an epidemic of mental health problems among older adults in the next century. Although 10 to 30% of older adults have emotional problems that are reversible when treated, less than 20% of older adults with a mental health diagnosis receive treatment (Koenig, 1994, p. 297). It is within this context that we provide a model intended to link diverse elders with faith organizations.

In an effort to identify the variations in perceptions of different position holders regarding the need for faith programs, the authors met with church leaders, congregation members, and agency leaders. During meetings with these various religious groups, the discussion often veered towards how a faith organization can begin to implement a community action program. Some scholars believe that church members, church leaders, social activists or academics should take responsibility for developing community action programs in faith organizations (Wineburg, 2001). Church leaders, academicians and social activists can be instrumental in providing needed knowledge and leadership but a significant barrier for these community activists has been the absence of a method to develop community action programs. The Faith-Based Community Action Model (FBCAM) was developed for that purpose.

The FBCAM includes concepts from community planning models but also includes methods that are specifically useful for faith organizations involved in community action planning. Included in the model are approaches to determining not only community needs but also assessment of values and attitudes essential for the successful planning of community action programs. Adapted from community organization principles, this twelve-step model provides faith organizations with a roadmap for planning community action programs targeted to diverse elders. Figure 1 provides an overview of the model.

In step one, the creation of a planning group is based on models that intend to develop the capacity of members to organize for change. In step two, a faith-based organization must determine its priorities and capabilities to undertake community action programs. The commitment of church leaders and parishioners is essential for success. Developing a network of relationships is based on coalition building principles for community action programs. Building a multi-organizational power base to influence program direction or draw on resources is essential in community planning. Planning a flexible agenda enhances the opportunity for community and congregational input thereby maximizing community acquiescence and ownership. Steps in defining the community problem to be addressed is basic community planning practice and deciding on a community action program with consensus and recognition of the limitations of resources is realistic social planning. Asking for commitment and support from key persons in the community and congregation insures a collaborative effort to support the project and insures resources will be available for the project. Involving community agencies develops additional resources from local government and state officials as well as community policy makers. Investigating other programs and involving other churches in the project insures political support from key community members rather than competition, duplication

FIGURE 1. The Faith-Based Community Action Model

Step 1: Form a planning group
Step 2: Define the church's mission in meeting community needs
Step 3: Develop a network of relationships
Step 4: Plan a flexible agenda
Step 5: Define the community problem
Step 6: Decide on a community action program
Step 7: Request commitments and support from key persons
Step 8: Involve community agencies
Step 9: Research similar programs sponsored by other churches
Step 10: Involve as many church members as possible
Step 11: Prepare alternative solutions
Step 12: Monitor, evaluate, and provide feedback

of services, and conflict. Formative and summative evaluation are key components of accountability and promote support for continuing action based programs.

Step One: Form a Planning Group

Determine the needs of the community and its interest in promoting community action programs. This planning group should include elders from diverse backgrounds so that from the very beginning their voices will be heard.

1. Invite community leaders, church leaders, and members of the congregation as key informants to discuss their views of community needs.

Step Two: Define the Church's Mission in Meeting the Community's Needs

Essential questions must be asked of congregations and church leaders regarding their willingness to become involved in community action programs. Older persons must be encouraged to express their views about how they perceive the role of the church within the community. If there are varied expectations about the church's mission, dialogue needs to occur here.

1. Determine if the church's mission is a social and/or spiritual mission.
2. Is this a civic oriented church?
3. Is this a church whose mission is evangelical and proselytizing?
4. Is the church leader willing to commit resources and time to social action programs?

Step Three: Develop a Network of Relationships

A network of relationships is essential for successful community action programs. This step requires inclusion of older persons in the network, as advisory board members but also as representatives of potential recipients of service.

1. Develop an advisory board of members. (Ten to fifteen are recommended for a cohesive group.)
2. Select members from the congregation, from other churches, from community agencies, and from business and political arenas.
3. Select those who are interested in community action and who are willing to commit time and resources to the project.

Step Four: Plan a Flexible Agenda

Being prepared with an agenda that includes examples of successful community action programs in comparable communities that can be used as a prototype is an effective method to garner support for the project. Knowing about successful projects and/or programs targeted to elders in local communities, and the roles played by faith organizations, will lend credence to the effort.

1. Develop an agenda of service needs for older persons in the community, but be prepared to change some of the program planning.
2. Be flexible and listen to community members.
3. Be open to what others have done within other communities, remembering that program design must be customized to the specific needs of your organization, its members, and its community.

Step Five: Define the Community Problems but Select One Problem for Action

After a comprehensive assessment of the community's needs, select one group and one problem for action. A lack of focus and resources that are not used wisely will contribute to failure. Given the diversity of elder needs, it will not always be possible to target "elders" generally. It may be more helpful to focus on groups within the elder population, perhaps groups with the greatest needs that you can address.

1. Define the community's needs but agree on one problem.

2. Do not try to solve all of the community's problems or all problems faced by elders.

3. Select one problem to be addressed and gather information from experts about causes and solutions.

Step Six: Decide on a Community Action Program

The experts in the community can provide information on successful and unsuccessful programs. Look to providers who have been sensitive to elders' needs and learn from their experiences. Decide on a program that is feasible at the present time. Remember that even if a program sounds wonderful, it may not be feasible given your faith organization's resources. Feasibility and fit must be assessed carefully so that elders' expectations are not falsely raised.

1. Select interested and knowledgeable volunteers from the community to take active roles in the implementation of the solution. For example, nurses, doctors, lawyers, social workers, and business leaders in the congregation can represent the professional community. Consumer representation is equally important.

2. Choose a community action program which a group decision supports.

Step Seven: Ask for Commitments and Support from Key Persons

When the program is selected, include as many members of the community as possible for supportive roles. Remember to think about diversity and the inclusion of elders.

1. Seek support from church administration for space, advertising, outreach efforts, volunteers, etc.

2. Use designated church space for meetings, etc.

3. Use newsletters to reach congregation for donations and volunteers and to provide on-going information about the program.

4. Use volunteers to help with securing community support.

Step Eight: Involve Community Agencies in the Planning Process

Community agencies are essential in providing additional services beyond the scope of faith organizations. Their collaboration is needed for success.

1. Involve a community agency and arrange for consultations by professionals for follow-up for referrals or treatment interventions.

2. Some examples are health screenings, medication checks, a mental health clinic, an Alzheimer's referral center, or a geriatric assessment clinic.

Step Nine: Investigate Other Churches, Synagogues, Temples, Mosques, etc., with Similar Programs

Learning from other programs avoids costly mistakes. Duplication of services is not cost effective. Replication of what is successful in one location must be tempered with what is known about the older population within the context of the local community. Programs designed with attention to unique community characteristics are essential.

1. Assess the possibility for collaboration and interfaith coalitions.
2. Investigate if there are similar programs in other neighborhoods or nearby cities.
3. Evaluate positive and negative consequences of collaboration with other groups.
4. Collect materials from other programs.
5. Visit other programs if possible.

Step Ten: Involve as Many Church Members as Possible in a Collaborative Coalition

Collaboration is key in community action programs. Involvement of members and community leaders is an essential ingredient to success. Engage leaders from among elders who will benefit from the program.

1. Present the plan to the community, to church members, and to decision-makers (i.e., local business leaders, local politicians, local senior citizens' groups, area agencies on aging, etc.).
2. Gather support from as many as possible.

Step Eleven: Prepare Alternative Solutions for Reaching the Goal

Alternative solutions may be necessary. Thinking about several ways to design the project or program means knowing about alternative models used by others. This method reinforces the importance of flexibility as noted earlier.

1. Have other options prepared and commitments from community providers for alternative solutions.
2. Spin scenarios of alternative proposals, with input from elders.

Step Twelve: Monitor, Evaluate, and Provide Feedback

Monitoring is necessary to evaluate project or program results. Positive and negative results must be provided to key players to determine if goals were met. Elder satisfaction must be a part of this process.

1. Provide feedback to church leaders, community planners, and community agencies.
2. Questions to ask are: how is the program working; what are the positives and negatives; why/why not is some aspect working/not working; how can these services be improved?

These twelve steps offer an approach for faith organizations to implement community action programs. This model incorporates basic principles of community planning and adapts these principles for faith organizations as they plan projects and programs for older adults in their community.

CONCLUSION:
RETURN TO THE HISTORICAL MISSION
OF THE CHURCH

In examining the rationale for the church as a service provider for older persons, the literature points to the failure of community agencies and the inability of government programs to provide needed social services. The religious community has the potential to develop partnerships with the neighborhood community, in order to address the needs of elders. While good intentions are critical, knowledge is essential. Collaboration can offer new opportunities to meet the needs of persons of all ages, especially older adults.

To date, organized religion has concentrated its outreach programs upon youth and families and ignored older persons. The diversity of the aging population and the variety of churches, synagogues, and mosques in various communities necessitates the need for programs that are unique to each community. Moberg (1991) suggests, "Every church needs to study its own community to determine the specific needs of its older people, and to identify the services that are already available to them, and to discern which are feasible but lacking" (p. 191). A sharing of knowledge about effective services and programs requires communication between religious leaders, organizations, congregants, and community providers. Religious organizations must again take on community, teaching, and leadership functions. Lack of lay leadership was found in a study by Tobin et al. (1986) to be a major barrier to program development. They found little collaboration between ecumenical groups and social service agencies in the community.

As federal policy shifts toward decentralization and the community is given more responsibility to provide services for its citizens, new collaborative models are mandated. The old ways are no longer suitable. New challenges require new efforts by the church and the government. The church and its prime resources, people, are in the provision of social services. Churches can offer services such as educational groups for health promotion, health counseling programs on alcohol drug abuse, and nutrition information. Most congregations include professionals such as doctors, nurses, social workers, health care workers, and pharmacists who can offer services to parishioners. An approach such as the faith-based community action model is one way to begin this process.

Korean churches are an example of faith organizations offering a wide range of services to their older adult members. Korean churches play a major role in the process of acculturation by providing socialization, information sharing, cultural activities, and other supportive functions for older adults.

The formal social service system is overburdened and is unable to cope with the expanding demand from a rapidly growing number of older adults. Thus, the challenge to restructure the formal service system leads one to examine the potential of untapped natural support systems, the thousands of faith organizations (churches, temples, mosques, synagogues). Faith-based initiatives are crucial in the 21st century.

REFERENCES

Atchley (1998). The importance of being religious. *American Society on Aging Newsletter*. March/April 9-12.

Billingsley, A. (1999). *Mighty like a river: The black church and social reform*. New York: Oxford University Press.

Bruggemann, W. G. (2002). *The practice of macro social work* (2nd ed.). New York: Brooks/Cole. 120-150.

Choy, B. (1979). *Koreans in America*. Chicago: Nelson Hall.

Choi, G. & Tirrito, T. (1999). The Korean church as a social service provider for older adults. *Arete, 23*(3), 69-83.

Cnaan, Ram A. (1997). Recognizing the role of religious congregations and denominations in social service provision. In Reisch, M. & Gambrill, E. (Eds.). *Social work in the 21st century.* 271-284. Thousand Oaks, CA: Pine Forge Press.

Cnaan, Ram with R. Wineburg & S. Boddie. (1999). *The newer deal: Social work and religion in partnership.* New York: Columbia University Press.

Durkheim, E. 1915. (1961). *The elementary forms of the religious life.* Translated by J.W. Swain. New York: Collier Books

Gulledge, Kirk J. (1992). Gerontological knowledge among clergy: Implications for seminary training. *Educational Gerontologist, 18,* 636-644.

Hungelmann, J., Kenkel-Rossi, E., Klassen, E., & Stollenwerk, R. (1996). Focus on spiritual well-being: Harmonious interconnectedness of mind-body-spirit–Use of the JAREL spiritual well-being scale. *Geriatric Nursing.* November/December, 262-266.

Hurh, W., & Kim, K. (1990). Religious participation of Korean immigrants in the United States. *Journal for the Scientific Study of Religion, 29*(1), 19-34.

Johnson, T. (1995). The significance of religion for aging well. *American Behavioral Scientist, 39*(2), 186-202.

Kim, B. (1979). Religious deprogramming & subjective reality. *Sociological Analysis, 140,* 3-10.

Koenig, H. G. (1994). *Aging and God.* 297-320. New York: The Haworth Press, Inc.

Koenig, H. G. (1995). *Research on religion and aging.* Westport, CT: Greenwood Press.

Koenig, H.G., George, L.K., & Schneider, R. (1994). Mental health care for older adults in the year 2020: A dangerous and avoided topic. *The Gerontologist, 34*(5), 674-679.

Koenig, H.G., George, L.K., & Seigler, I.C. (1988). The use of religion and other emotion-regulating coping strategies among older adults. *The Gerontologist, 28,* 303-310.

Koenig, H.G., & Weaver, L. (1998). Religion provides counseling tool. *American Society on Aging Newsletter.* 9-12.

Krause, N. (1991). Religion, aging and health: Current status and future prospects. *Journal of Gerontology. 52 B.* (6) 291-293.

Levin, J.S. & Markides, K.S. (1985). Religion and health in Mexican-Americans. *Journal of Religion and Health. 24.*60-69.

Lewis, M. (1994). Religious congregations and the informal supports of the frail elderly. Project summary. New York: Fordham University. 1-39.

Logan, S. (1996). *The black family: Strengths, self-help, and positive change.* Boulder, CO: Westview.

Moberg, D. O. (1991). Preparing for the graying of the church. *Review and Expositor, 88,* 179-192.

Netting, F.E. (1984). Church-related agencies and social welfare. *Social Service Review, 58*(3), 404-420.

Netting, F., Thibault, J., & Ellor, J. (1988). Spiritual integration: Gerontological interface between the religious and social service communities. *Journal of Religion & Aging 5*(1/2), 61-74.

Petersen, J., & Lee, G. (1975). Religious affiliation and social participation: Differences between Lutherans and Catholics. *Journal of Voluntary Action Research, 8*(2), 82-94.

Reid, D., Linder, R., Shelley, B., & Stout, H. (1990). *The dictionary of Christianity in America.* Downers Grove, IL: Intervarsity Press.

Simmons, H.C. (1991). Ethical perspectives on church and synagogue as intergenerational support systems. *Journal of Religious Gerontology, 7*(4),17-28.

Sherman, L., & Viggiani, P. (1996). The impact of federal policy changes on children: Research needs for the future. *Social Work, 41*(6), 594-600.

Smith, J. M. (1993). Function and supportive roles of church and religion. In J. Jackson, L. Chatters, & R. Taylor (Eds.), *Aging in Black America.* 90-120. Newbury Park, CA: Sage.

Taylor, R. (1993). Religion and Religious Observances. In J. Jackson, L. Chatters, & R. Taylor. (Eds.). *Aging in Black America.* 50-100. Newbury Park, CA: Sage Publications.

Thompson, W., Streib, G., & Kosa, J. (1960). The effect of retirement on personal adjustment: A panel analysis. *Journal of Gerontology, 15*, 165-169.

Tirrito, T. & Euster, G. (1994). Religious leaders: What do they need to know about planning for elderly church members? Paper presented at the Association for Gerontology in Higher Education. Cleveland, Ohio, Feb. 1-5

Tirrito, T. & Spencer-Amado, J. (2000). Older Adults Willingness to Use Social Services in Places of Worship. *Journal of Religious Gerontology. 11*(2), 29-42.

Tobin, S. (1995). Older Americans as a resource. In T. Tedrick (Ed). *Aging: Issues and policies for the 80s.* New York. Praeger Press.

Tobin, S., Ellor, J.W., & Anderson-Ray, S. (1986). *Enabling the elderly: Religious institutions within the community service system.* Albany, NY: State University of New York Press.

U.S. Census. 2000. Washington, D.C. Population Estimates. Population Division. http://www.census.gov/population/estimates/nation/infile2-1.txt.

Wineburg, B. (2001). *A limited partnership: The politics of religion, welfare and social service.* New York: Columbia University Press.

Zucker, D.K., Fair, F.A., & Branchley, L.V. (1987). Associations between patient religiosity and alcohol attitudes and knowledge in an alcohol treatment program. *The International Journal of Addictions.* 47-53.

The Heritage of Religion and Spirituality in the Field of Gerontology: Don Clingan, Tom Cook, and the National Interfaith Coalition on Aging

James W. Ellor, PhD
Melvin A. Kimble, PhD

SUMMARY. This article presents the history of the National Interfaith Coalition on Aging. This organization, like many, owes its founding to many important people. Two key individuals are Donald Clingan and Thomas Cook, Jr. To understand the history of this organization is to understand the labors of these two witnesses. The authors interviewed these two men in order to both celebrate their contributions to this orga-

Rev. James W. Ellor is Director of the Institute of Gerontological Studies at Baylor University School of Social Work, Waco, Texas. He is also Associate Director of the Center for Aging, Religion and Spirituality, St. Paul, MN. The Rev. Melvin A. Kimble, PhD, is Professor Emeritus at Luther Seminary, St. Paul, MN. He is the Director of the Center for Aging, Religion and Spirituality, St. Paul, MN.

The authors would like to recognize and thank the Retirement Research Foundation for the funding that made the original interviews found in this article possible. They would also like to thank James S. Seeber for his contributions to the Clingan interview.

It should be noted that immediately prior to the publication of this article, Tom Cook was kind enough to read it over to insure accuracy. Unfortunately, Don Clingan had already died, so was unable to do so.

[Haworth co-indexing entry note]: "The Heritage of Religion and Spirituality in the Field of Gerontology: Don Clingan, Tom Cook, and the National Interfaith Coalition on Aging." Ellor, James W., and Melvin A. Kimble. Co-published simultaneously in *Journal of Religious Gerontology* (The Haworth Pastoral Press, an imprint of The Haworth Press, Inc.) Vol. 16, No. 1/2, 2004, pp. 143-153; and: *Faith-Based Initiatives and Aging Services* (ed: F. Ellen Netting, and James W. Ellor) The Haworth Pastoral Press, an imprint of The Haworth Press, Inc., 2004, pp. 143-153. Single or multiple copies of this article are available for a fee from The Haworth Document Delivery Service [1-800-HAWORTH, 9:00 a.m. - 5:00 p.m. (EST). E-mail address: docdelivery@haworthpress.com].

http://www.haworthpress.com/web/JRG
Digital Object Identifier: 10.1300/J078v16n01_10

nization as well as to fully understand the history of this important organization. *[Article copies available for a fee from The Haworth Document Delivery Service: 1-800-HAWORTH. E-mail address: <docdelivery@haworthpress.com> Website: <http://www.HaworthPress.com> © 2004 by The Haworth Press, Inc. All rights reserved.]*

KEYWORDS. Spiritual well-being, religion, aging, White House Conference on Aging, church

Embedded within the workings of any important organization or national movement are the lives of significant people without whom the organization or movement would have never existed. When an individual invests in a group of people or in a concept, his or her life enriches those touched by the organization that emerges. As beneficiaries of the work of the hands of such persons, the world can appreciate the products, the organizations or ideas furthered by their labors. Yet, too often, the lives of those responsible are lost. In this way organizations and movements that flourish are like an attractive quilt. Hundreds of years after it is painstakingly sewn, it hangs on a wall. The quilt is appreciated, but what of the quilter?

In 1996 Jim Ellor and Mel Kimble of the Center for Aging, Religion and Spirituality became aware of the frailty of some of the key players in the origination of studies in religion and spirituality and aging. With the aid of a grant from the Retirement Research Foundation, Jim and Mel set about interviewing as many of these key people as possible. Many of these pioneers have now died, but in the pages of this article we have attempted to share their story as well as some of the impacts each had on the field. Each of these interviews was conducted with a previously designed set of questions that were supplied to the interviewee ahead of time. However, each was also allowed to add his or her own concerns to the dialogue. These interviews were conducted between 1995 and 1996. Most were face-to-face; however, three were done by phone.

In an effort to offer a more readable format, the results of these interviews have been combined by topic. In this article, the stories of Don Clingan and Thomas Cook will be shared along with the history of the National Interfaith Coalition on Aging to which both contributed. The National Interfaith Coalition on Aging (NICA) is now a constituent unit of the National Council on the Aged (NCOA). However, it originated out of the 1971 White House Conference on Aging and labored as an independent organization for over twenty years before it merged to become a part of NCOA. The work of these two men and this organization offer important insights into the history and development of one piece of the puzzle that is the history of research and program development in religion, spirituality and aging. It should be noted, however, that while these two individuals were significant, they did not work alone, but rather with a large number of other hard working people.

TWO MEN, ONE IMPORTANT MISSION

Neither Don Clingan nor Tom Cook set out early in their careers to work with older adults. Both were called to the ordained ministry, one in the Disciples of Christ and the other the Presbyterian Church. Each moved from parish ministry to programmatic employment and finally into gerontology. The following is a sketch of the lives of each of these important people.

Rev. Donald F. Clingan, D.Min.

Don was born in Atchison, Kansas, of Atchison, Topeka, Santa Fe Railroad fame, on February 25, 1926. He and his family lived in Atchison for a few years, and then his father, who was a credit manager for a wholesale hardware company, was transferred to Wichita, Kansas. Don attended the first part of grade school there, but then the depression came along and the company went bankrupt. His father had to start over again. He became the assistant credit manager for Lee Wholesale Hardware Company in Salina, Kansas. Don finished grade school and high school in Salina, Kansas. After graduation he had two years in the Army/Air Force just after World War II. When he returned, he went to Phillips University in Enid, Oklahoma, where he received a Bachelor of Arts degree. He then served for two years as an Associate Minister or Director of Religious Education for the Hillside Christian Church in Wichita, Kansas. He then went to Brite Divinity School at Texas Christian University. He received a Bachelor of Divinity degree, which later was re-issued as the Master of Divinity degree from Brite Divinity School at Texas Christian University.

Later, after he became so involved in the field of ministry with the aging, he decided to go back for his Doctor of Ministry degree. Don received his Doctorate from Christian Theological Seminary, but he did it in ministry with the aging and Christian ethics. After his emersion into the field of gerontology, Don took work at the University of Oregon Center for Gerontology in Eugene and also at the New England Gerontology Center at the University of New Hampshire in Durham.

Don moved from his work as a parish pastor of a small church in rural Oklahoma and Kansas in the 1950s to become the Director of Program Planning for the Department of World Outreach Education of the Division of Homeland Ministries of the Christian Church, Disciples of Christ in 1965. After a couple of years in this position, Don moved to a new position as the Assistant to the Vice President and Director of services to the Congregation for National Benevolence Association (NBA) of the Christian Church, Disciples of Christ in order to support their new emphasis on congregations. It was in this capacity that Don was selected to be one of over 60 denominational representatives to the 1971 White House Conference on Aging.

Prior to the 1971 White House Conference, a pre-conference was organized for the over 300 national voluntary organizations that would be represented at the White House Conference in order to organize and prepare the representatives of these organizations. Don was also selected for this group. The National Voluntary Organizations for Independent Living for Aging or what became known as N-Voila, was an important link for Don. This was his first real immersion beyond his parish experience into gerontology. Don notes that Arthur Flemming was very interested in the voluntary sector and religious movements involved in the White House Conference, but since he was the chair of the entire conference, he appointed Dr. Ellen Winston to Chair N-Voila.

It turned out that Roger Carstensen and Tom Cook were also involved in N-Voila and they along with Thomas W. Mahler, director of the Kellogg Center for Continuing Education, and Dr. David Levine, of the department of social work, at the University of Georgia, contacted Don to further the collaboration for the religious sector. These individuals became a working team prior to the White House Conference, contacting various leaders of the denominations who would be present about their interest in aging. Even prior to the actual White House Conference, Don Clingan, Roger Carstensen and Tom Cook were posing the question as to the need for a National-Interfaith group that would involve more directly the various religious traditions and their work with older adults. Sister Marie Gaffney from the National Conference of Catholic Charities, Dr. David L. Levine, from the University of Georgia and representatives of many Protestant Christian, Roman Catholic and Jewish faith traditions along with Dr. Bernard Nash, Executive Director

of the National Retired Teachers Association and American Association of Retired Persons, were involved in this first dialogue.

The Spiritual Well-Being section of the 1971 White House Conference was one of the keys to this initiative. While the 1951 and 1961
White House Conferences on Aging had called this a religious section,
the 1971 conference referred to it by a new name, the Spiritual Well-Being Section. At the meetings of this section even more contacts were
made and the resolution to follow up on the work of this group with a
new national movement was declared. The White House Conference
was held in December of 1971 and the first Interfaith Conference was
held soon thereafter–March 8-10, 1972. This important event had about
forty people present along with a reporter from the *Christian Century.*
Sessions were held at the U.GA. Center for Continuing Education and
at the Christian College of Georgia in Athens, Georgia. It was hosted by
Roger Carstensen, then President of Christian College of Georgia. Dr.
Carstensen and Don Clingan were the co-chairs of this event.

At this event, the group set four objectives for the new organization:

- To identify and give priority to those programs and services for the
  aging which may best be implemented through the resources of the
  nation's religious sector;
- To vitalize and develop the role of the church and synagogue with
  respect to their responsibility in improving the quality of life for
  the aging;
- To stimulate cooperation and coordinated action between the nation's religious sector and national secular private and public organizations and agencies whose programs and services relate to the
  welfare and dignity of older persons.
- To encourage the aging to continue giving to society from the
  wealth of their experiences and to remain active participants in
  community life. (Evans, 2004, p. 2)

From this initial meeting, a second meeting was held on August 1-2,
1972 in the offices of the National Center for Voluntary Action in
Washington D.C. This meeting was called to bring together all of the
national religious bodies to further discuss an interfaith coalition to
work toward the support of older adults in religious settings. While attending this event, Don Clingan was selected as the first President of the
new National Interfaith Coalition on Aging. Three Vice Presidents were
also selected, Dr. John McDowell of the National Council of Churches,
to represent the Protestant Faiths; Sister Irene Seebo, OSB of the United

States Catholic Conference, to represent the Roman Catholic traditions; and Dr. David L. Levine from the University of Georgia Council on Gerontology to represent the Jewish traditions. They then decided that rather than a secretary and treasurer, they would have a Director of the Secretariat. Dr. Roger Carstensen of the Christian College of Georgia was elected to this position. The new organization was incorporated in Washington D.C. on April 17, 1973.

Tom Cook, according to Dr. Clingan, was a "marvel" at writing grant proposals (Ellor, 1996a, p. 12). Tom drafted the first grant for NICA in late 1972. Tom was able to give up his work with the Athens Community Council on Aging to become the Project Director for NICA. The first grant was received on January 7, 1973. During these first two years, Don and Tom worked together on many things. Don focused on building the organization from his office in Indianapolis, Indiana and Tom on the grant activities from his office in Athens, Georgia. Don noted in his interview that the National Benevolence Association of the Christian Church, Disciples of Christ contributed a lot to the making of NICA in those early days, not the least of which was his time. This was the contribution of William T. Gibble, Don's supervisor at that time. Dr. Gibble in April of 1975 agreed that Don should become the part-time Executive Director of NICA. It was also in fall 1975 that Don premiered the first edition of his book, *Aging Persons in the Community of Faith* (Clingan, 1975). This book was designed to be a congregational guide for interfaith programming with older adults and a support for NICA as it was growing into its role as a recognized leader in this field. When Don became the new Executive Director of NICA, J. Watson of the United Church of Christ became the second President of the NICA Board.

These were fruitful times at NICA. In 1975 the definition of Spiritual Well-being was developed in anticipation of the 1976 inter-decade Interfaith Conference on Aging. The newsletter *NICA Inform* was first developed and distributed, the movie *The Third Age: The New Generation,* starring Irene Tidrow was developed with help from the National Benevolence Association and NICA, and the important research involving contacts within 106 national religious bodies as to the role of the church in providing services for the aged was being conducted by Tom Cook.

At this same time, Don developed the National Center for Ministry with the Aging, as the focus for his work with the National Benevolence Association. Through this center, Don was able to offer workshops, develop print materials and organize a speaker's bureau. The two tandem positions offered Don a basis for his ministry until 1984 when cutbacks forced him to leave these positions and return to the parish. Don and his family moved to the First Christian Church of Springfield, Illinois in 1984 where he was the senior pastor until 1992 when he retired. This was not the final chapter for Don, however, as he returned to the NICA Board for one term from 1998 to 2003 and chaired the nominations committee for part of that time.

Don Clingan died in February 2004. It was said of Don, that the four most important things in his life were his family, the Bible, music, and NICA. During the time that he actively served the coalition, Don often "was" NICA. It was clearly his heartfelt ministry. It was also said at his funeral that one could expect to receive a hug from Don anytime one saw him. The pastor that conducted the memorial service noted that he was sure that Don was greeting St. Peter with the phrase, "come on over here and give me a big hug!" He noted that Don was privileged to be a pioneer in his field and a critical part of the history of the National Interfaith Coalition on Aging.

Rev. Thomas Cook, Jr., M.A., M.Div.

The Reverend Thomas Cook, Jr. was born in Richmond, Virginia. At the time his family had just moved to Salisbury, North Carolina, but his mother returned to Richmond as that is where her doctor was as well as the family tradition. All the members of the Cook family were born in Richmond. His family later moved to Lawrence, South Carolina where Tom went to High School. Tom went to the Presbyterian College in Clinton, South Carolina. During college Tom reports that he was there to please his parents, so he was not clear as to what he wanted to do. He notes that his brother, father and grandfather were all Presbyterian Ministers, so he felt that he was expected to be one also. However, he was less clear on that point. Following his second year of college, Tom enrolled at the University of Geneva in Switzerland in the school of architecture, but since Presbyterian College did not have an architecture program, he finished his undergraduate degree there in 1955 with a major in French and a minor in Sociology. Tom was also commissioned Second Lieutenant in the U.S. Army Security Agency as a reserve officer. It was during this period, awaiting special language studies at Fort Devens MA. that he found his call to ministry. Tom finished his Master's of Divinity Degree at Union Theological Seminary in Richmond, Virginia along with an M.A. in Greek Bible and the Masters of Christian Education from the Presbyterian School of Christian Education, where he met his wife.

Upon completing graduate studies, Tom aspired to become a missionary in Korea, so he sought further training while serving as chaplain and bible teacher at Chamberlayne-Hunt academy in Port Gibson, Mississippi. Subsequently, in a change of course he went on to a pastorate in Stuttgart, Arkansas. While en route to attend his grandmother's funeral, he passed through Atlanta. His brother's wife, who worked for Senior Citizen's Services of Metropolitan Atlanta, urged him to take a position with the Title III program there. Tom was eyed for director of the new Athens Community Council on aging, a fledgling Title III Program. He combined programs there with the Model Cities Program in that area. Along with this he also served as consultant with an office in the Georgia Commission on Aging under outgoing Governor Maddox and later under the office of Governor Jimmy Carter.

When asked how he got involved in the field of Gerontology, Tom notes, "I think a lot of us enter the field not because we feel that intense interest or knowledge or understanding, but for many, almost like the accident of birth, you know. I have always had a very strong affinity to older adults. This is much more with NICA, than other age groups. I think partly this is the result of the fact that my maternal grandmother had been orphaned." Tom's grandmother, her sister and brother, were orphaned from a very early age. Her grandparents raised them out in the country in a day when there was not the communications and media that we have today. So she was raised by an older generation. She married a man who was twenty years her senior. Tom continued, "I guess in those days it was fairly common in some ways. But growing up, for instance, my language was not the language of my parents' generation, although they were raised of course with that same language. I knew a bicycle as a 'wheel,' which of course goes back to the much earlier version of the large wheeled vehicle. A refrigerator was an 'icebox,' and all kinds of expressions that were common in an earlier age. My grandmother often said 'It is as cold as a froe.'" A 'froe' is the tool used to split shingles and commonly used to split firewood and kindling. You would go out into the cold to do it and the metal could get pretty cold. And whole bunch of folklore came to me from that skipped generation so that I related very easily to older persons in the church and it was just a natural sort of thing for me" (Ellor, 1996b, 16).

Tom moved to Athens, Georgia to direct the Athens Community Council on Aging and as a consultant for the Georgia Commission on Aging. There he met Roger Carstensen, President of the Christian College of Georgia. It was also through this work with the Title III programs that he met David Levine, Professor of Social Work at the University of Georgia.

Immediately after the December White House Conference on Aging, Tom, Don, and Roger Carstensen began their work to develop NICA. Don Clingan in his own History of the Interfaith Movement (Gentzler and Clingan, 1996, 126-127) points to the three significant projects of the National Interfaith Coalition as being:

1. Survey of Aging Programs Under Religious Auspices
2. Project GIST (Gerontology in Seminary Training)
3. The various Conferences, including the Intra-Decade Conference in Atlanta, in 1976.

(It was from this conference that Tom and James Thorson contributed to, edited and published the book *Spiritual Well-Being of the Elderly*, bringing a wide range of viewpoints from religious sector writers.)

Tom was not present at the White House Conference of 1971, but he was a key player in Chicago when the interfaith representatives met to develop the definition of Spiritual Well-being in advance of the Inter-Decade meeting in Atlanta on Spiritual Well-Being. He was also present for the 1981 White House Conference that focused more on Ethics rather than religion or spiritual well-being.

As the funding for NICA began to run out, Tom became a consultant to the Robert Wood Johnson Foundation as they developed the Interfaith Caregiver programs. Later he became Minister of Congregational Care at the huge Highland Park Presbyterian Church in Dallas, TX. Tom was a founding board member of the Mission for Biblical Literacy, Inc. and during his 25 years in that organization served as editor of Biblical Literacy Today, and became Project Minister for Israel and Liaison to the House of Hope International Peace Center in the Holy Land. Retired from the active parish, Tom and his wife Wanda serve as peacemakers in the Middle East. Tom has now completed over 32 mission trips in the past 14 years and continues to write, edit and speak on both aging and peacemaking. He says, "NICA was a training ground for me in ecumenicity. Today all of my experience in organizational development, working with people from different traditions and theological backgrounds as well as every skill I learned directing NICA for those important years is of great value in the efforts I put forth in peacemaking at the grass-roots as well as the international level" (Ellor, 1996b). Today Tom has become involved at every judicatory level in the Presbyterian Church (USA)'s peacemaking and justice sections. Tom was a key player at an important time in the interfaith movement. Like Don Clingan he was a pioneer in our field.

The National-Interfaith Coalition on Aging

The National-Interfaith Coalition on Aging has benefited from the labors of many hands. Key figures like Thomas Robb, John Evans and Rita Chow have followed Don and Tom as staff persons for NICA. Each person left their mark. From it's inception just prior to the 1971 White House conference on Aging NICA has focused on offering a place for the various religious denominations to come together to celebrate and enhance their work on behalf of the religious and spiritual needs of older adults. In the beginning, only denominations could be members of NICA. It was not until 1975 that NICA began to allow affiliate members to join NICA. This status was upgraded to individual members in 1978 and continues to this day. Over the years the role of the denominations has moved from being the only focus of NICA, to being a key focus among other groups. This reflects in part the fact that today, there are few persons within the various denominations who have the elderly as more than a minor part of their job description.

In 1991, the NICA board voted to join the National Council on the Aging (NCOA) as a Constituent Unit. Rev. John Evans became the staff person and initiated their Clergy Leadership Project, which had funding from the Administration on Aging to produce materials that could help to develop programs for older adults in congregations. Today, NICA continues to be a constituent unit of NCOA. Rita Chow, Ph.D., RN, is the part-time staff person. At the meeting in April of 2004, the final vestiges in the Bylaws that suggested that the Denominational representatives had to constitute a percentage of the Delegate Council were removed. Today, NICA is focused for the future to continue to support denominations, organizations and individuals seeking to serve the spiritual and religious needs of older adults.

CONCLUSION

The National Interfaith Coalition on Aging owes its existence to a great many pilgrims on the road to fulfill a mission that began just prior to the 1971 White House Conference on Aging and continues today. Two key pioneers were Don Clingan and Thomas Cook, Jr. Both Don and Tom were born at a time when World War II was a part of their adolescence. Both served in the Army and both heard the call to professional ministry, one in the Christian Church, Disciples of Christ and one to the then Presbyterian Church, U.S. (This denomination merged in 1983 with the United Presbyterian Church, U.S.A. into the current Presbyterian Church, U.S.A.). Both served local congregations before becoming involved in the work of an agency. For both Don and Tom, the key to their emergence into the field of religions, spirituality and aging, was the 1971 White House Conference on Aging. These two men made different contributions, but together have served valuable functions to advance the field. They are true pioneers in our collective journey to serve the spiritual and religious needs of older adults.

REFERENCES

Clingan, D. F. (1975). *Aging Persons in the Community of Faith*. St. Louis: Christian Board of Publication.

Ellor, J. W., & Kimble, M. A. (1996a). CARS History Project, Interview with Don Clingan. In J. W. Ellor & M. A. Kimble (Eds.). St. Paul: Center for Aging Religion and Spirituality.

Ellor, J. W., & Kimble, M. A. (1996b). CARS History Project Interview with Thomas Cook, Jr. In J. W. Ellor & M. A. Kimble (Eds.). St. Paul: Center for Aging Religion and Spirituality.

Evans, J. (2004). *The Foundation of NICA's Beginnings*. Washington D.C.: National Interfaith Coalition on Aging.

Gentzler, R. H., & Clingan, D. F. (1996). *Aging: God's Challenge to Church & Synagogue*. Nashville: Disciples Resources.

Index

Abortion, 3
Abstinence-based programs,
    secularization of, 75-76
Accountability
    of faith-based initiatives/social
      services, 73
    in volunteerism, 110
    in volunteer management of older
      adults, 110,114-117,119-120
Acquired immunodeficiency syndrome
    (AIDS) organizations, 51
Addams, Jane, 41
Adler, Alfred, 23
Administration on Aging,
    56-57,59-60,152
Advocacy, 32
Afghanistan War, 16-17,18
African-American churches, 126
Aging Persons in the Community of
    Faith (Clingan), 148
AIDS organizations, 51
Aid to Families with Dependent
    Children (AFDC), 54
Al-Anon, 126
Alateen, 126
Alcohol abuse
    negative correlation with
      religiousness, 129
    undertreatment in older adults, 133
Alcoholics Anonymous (AA), 126,127
American Association of Retired
    Persons, 146-147
Anabaptists, 4-5
Anglican Church/Anglicans, 5-6,7,8,85
Annals of the American Academy of
    Political and Social Science,
    41
Anti-Semitism, 45
Area Agency on Aging, 59-60

Ashcroft, John, 54
Aspen Institute, 101
Association for Research on Nonprofit
    Organizations, 110
Association for Volunteer
    Administration, 110
Athens (Georgia) Community Council
    on Aging, 148,150-151
Authority, civil *versus* religious, 3-4

Backus, Isaac, 84,85
Baptist Community Services,
    Amarillo, Texas, 91-92
Baptist General Convention of Texas
    (BGCT), 89-92,96
    child welfare organizations
      affiliated with, 90-91,95
    Christian Life Commission, 85,96
    Human Care Ministry Website,
      89,91
    senior adult programs, 91-95,96
Baptist Joint Committee on Public
    Affairs (BJC), 86,87,88
Baptist Memorial Ministries, 91-92,96
Baptists, 8,113
    dogma of, 83
    faith-based initiatives and, 81-98
    historical background of,
      82-83,84-85
    religious liberty and, 83,84-85
    worldwide number of, 82-83
Baylor University, Dawson Institute of
    Church-State Studies, 87
Biblical Literacy Today, 151
Bill of Rights, 6-7,85
Blood transfusions, 3,6
Bone v. *Kendrick,* 75-76

BOOK ORDER FORM!

Order a copy of this book with this form or online at:
http://www.haworthpress.com/store/product.asp?sku=5458

Faith-Based Initiatives and Aging Services

_____ in softbound at $19.95 (ISBN: 0-7890-2734-8)
_____ in hardbound at $34.95 (ISBN: 0-7890-2733-X)

COST OF BOOKS _____	❏**BILL ME LATER:**
	Bill-me option is good on US/Canada/
POSTAGE & HANDLING _____	Mexico orders only; not good to jobbers,
US: $4.00 for first book & $1.50	wholesalers, or subscription agencies.
for each additional book	
Outside US: $5.00 for first book	❏**Signature** _____
& $2.00 for each additional book.	
	❏ **Payment Enclosed: $** _____
SUBTOTAL _____	
	❏ **PLEASE CHARGE TO MY CREDIT CARD:**
In Canada: add 7% GST _____	
STATE TAX _____	❏ Visa ❏ MasterCard ❏ AmEx ❏ Discover
CA, IL, IN, MN, NJ, NY, OH & SD residents	❏ Diner's Club ❏ Eurocard ❏ JCB
please add appropriate local sales tax.	**Account #**_____
FINAL TOTAL _____	**Exp Date** _____
If paying in Canadian funds, convert	
using the current exchange rate,	**Signature** _____
UNESCO coupons welcome.	_(Prices in US dollars and subject to change without notice.)_

PLEASE PRINT ALL INFORMATION OR ATTACH YOUR BUSINESS CARD

Name

Address

City   State/Province   Zip/Postal Code

Country

Tel   Fax

E-Mail

May we use your e-mail address for confirmations and other types of information? ❏Yes ❏No We appreciate receiving your e-mail address. Haworth would like to e-mail special discount offers to you, as a preferred customer. **We will never share, rent, or exchange your e-mail address.** We regard such actions as an invasion of your privacy.

Order From Your **Local Bookstore** or Directly From
The Haworth Press, Inc. 10 Alice Street, Binghamton, New York 13904-1580 • USA
Call Our toll-free number (1-800-429-6784) / Outside US/Canada: (607) 722-5857
Fax: 1-800-895-0582 / Outside US/Canada: (607) 771-0012
E-mail your order to us: orders@haworthpress.com

For orders outside US and Canada, you may wish to order through your local
sales representative, distributor, or bookseller.
For information, see http://haworthpress.com/distributors

(Discounts are available for individual orders in US and Canada only, not booksellers/distributors.)

Please photocopy this form for your personal use.
www.HaworthPress.com

BOF05